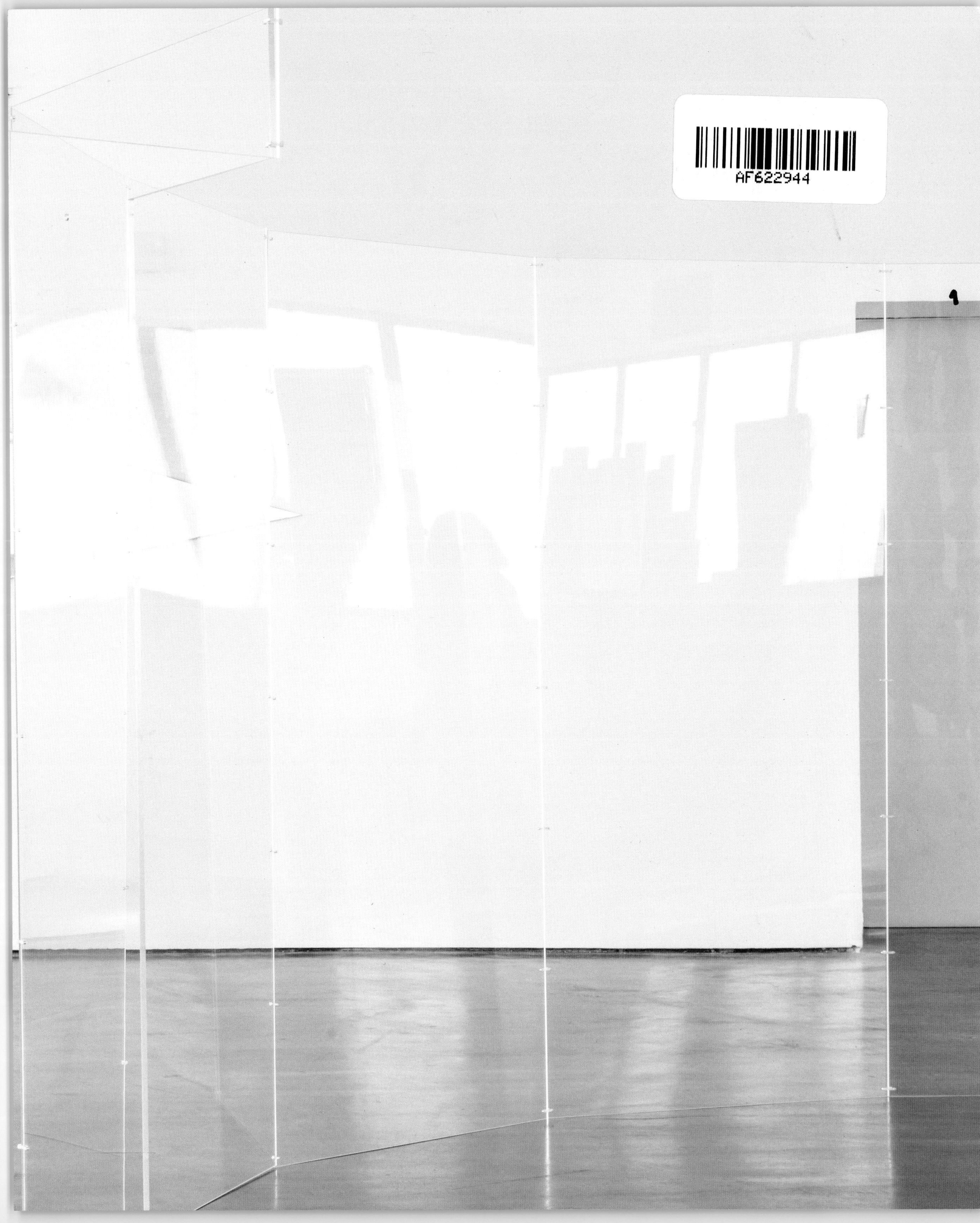

2

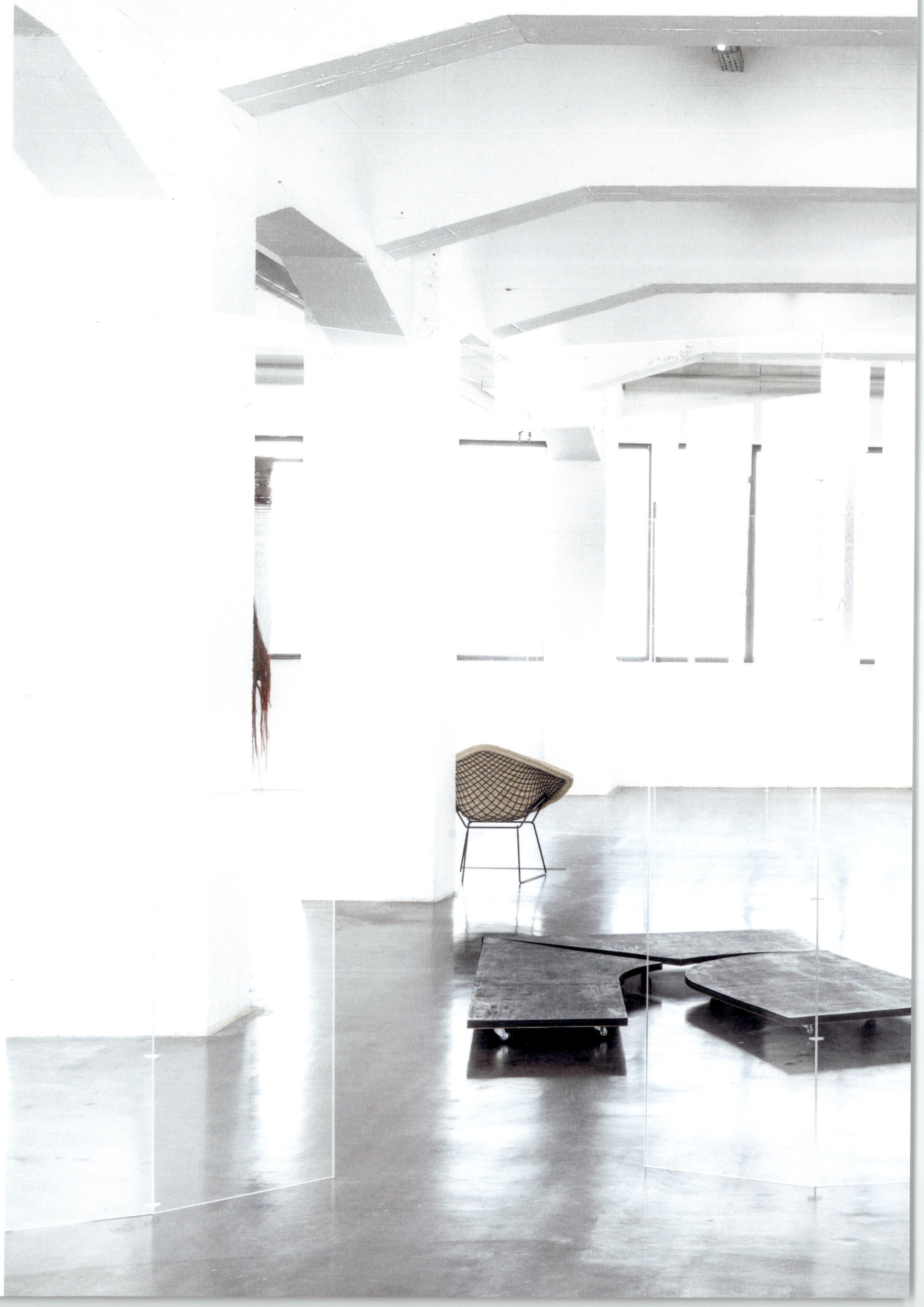

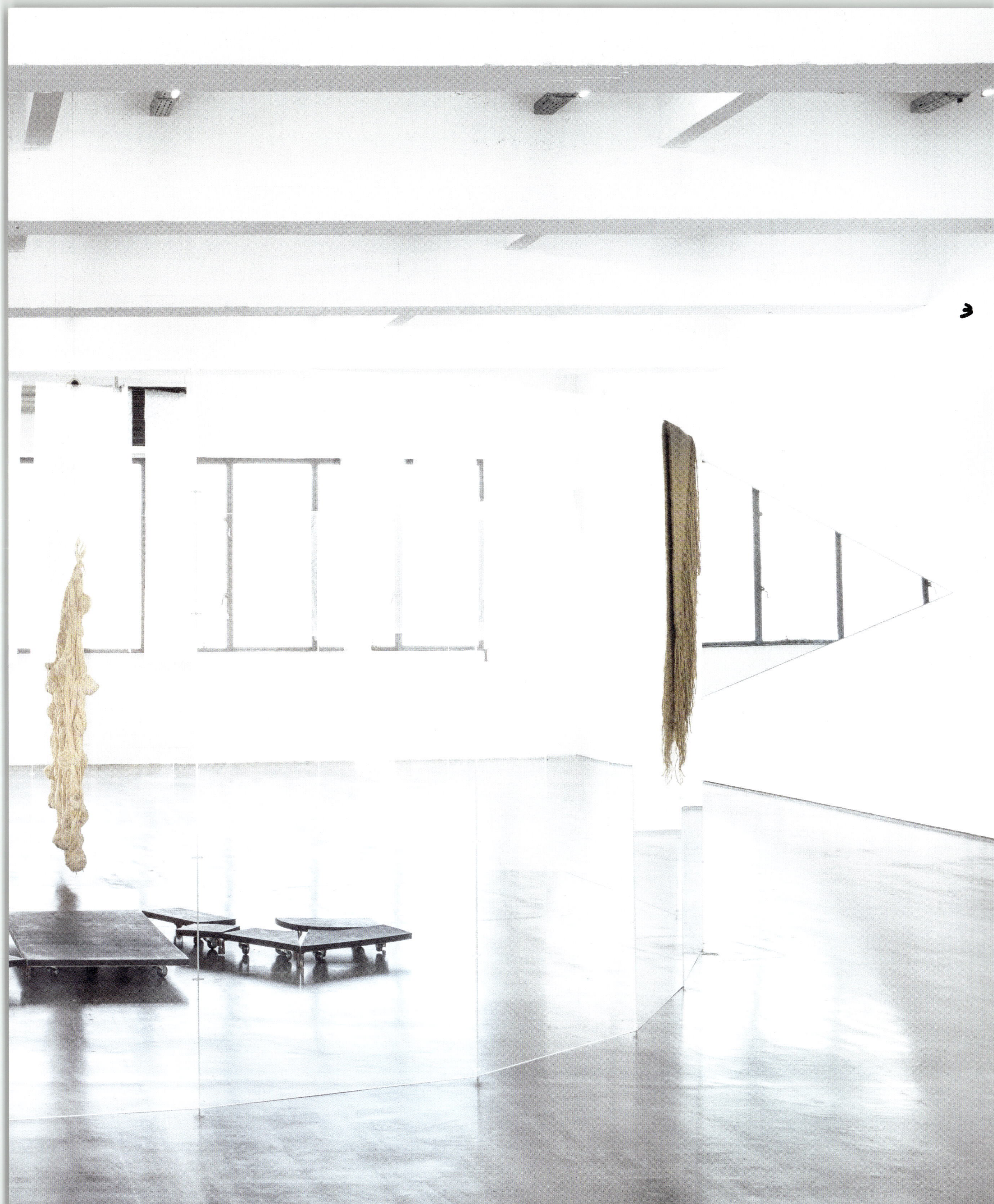

4

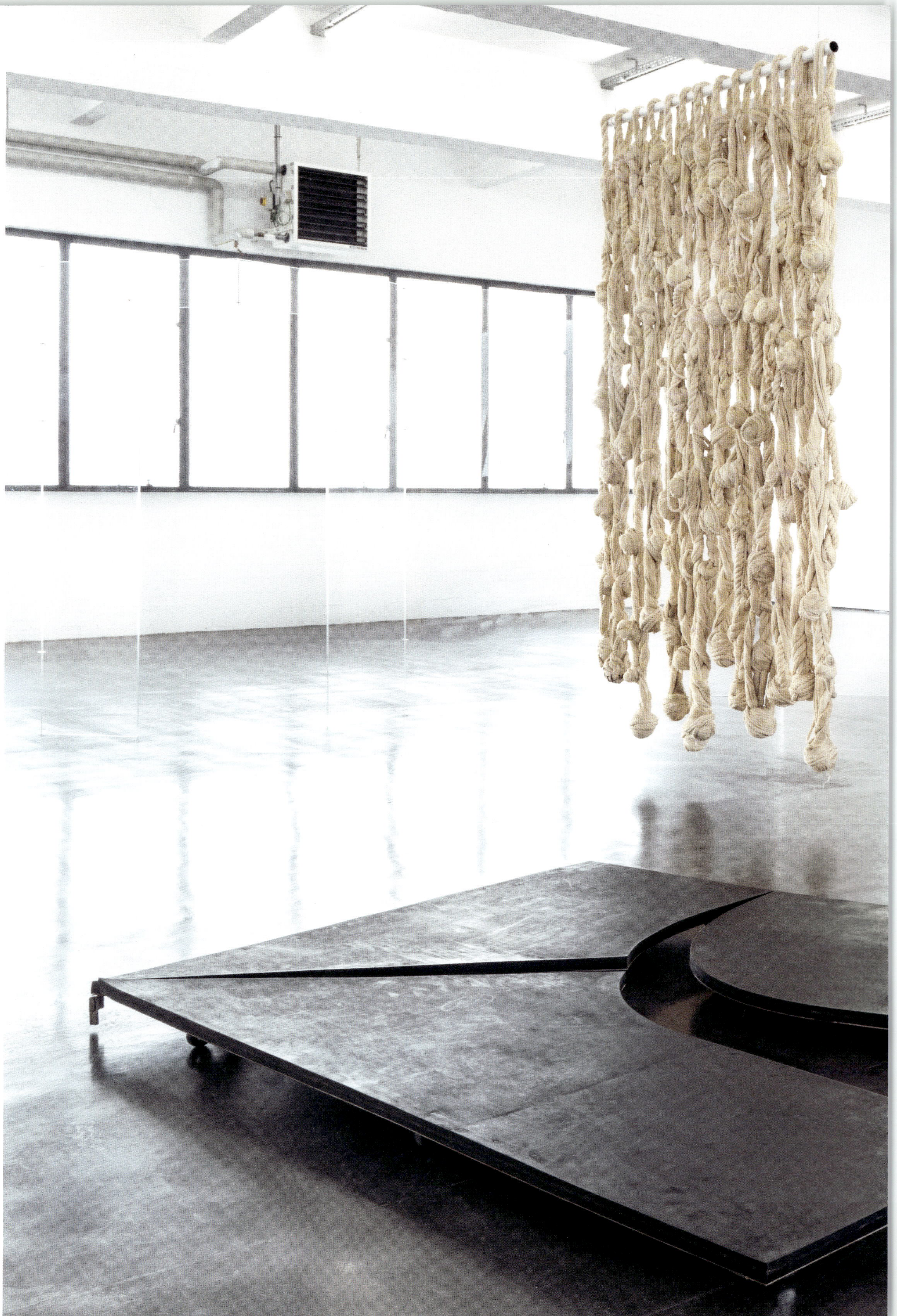

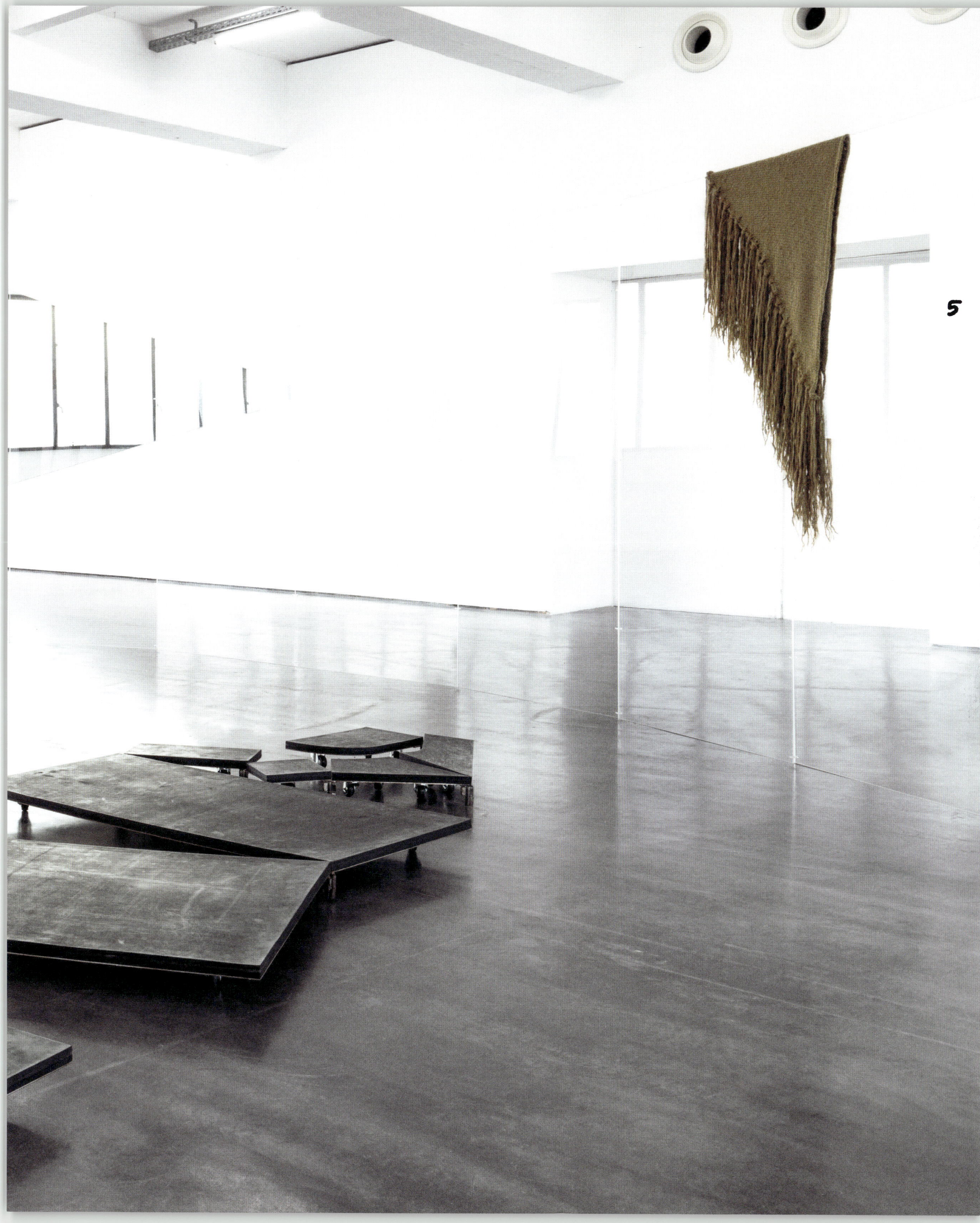

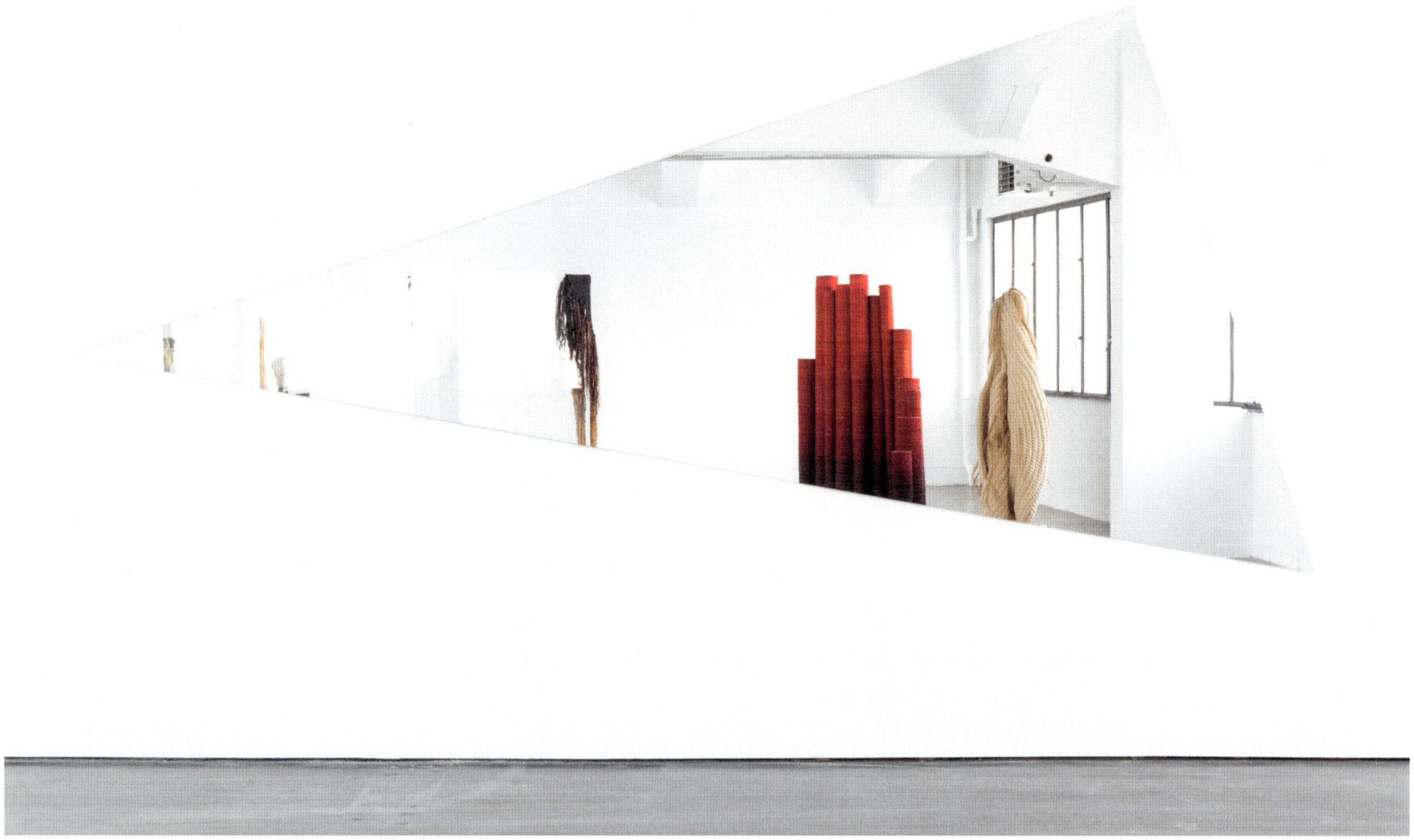

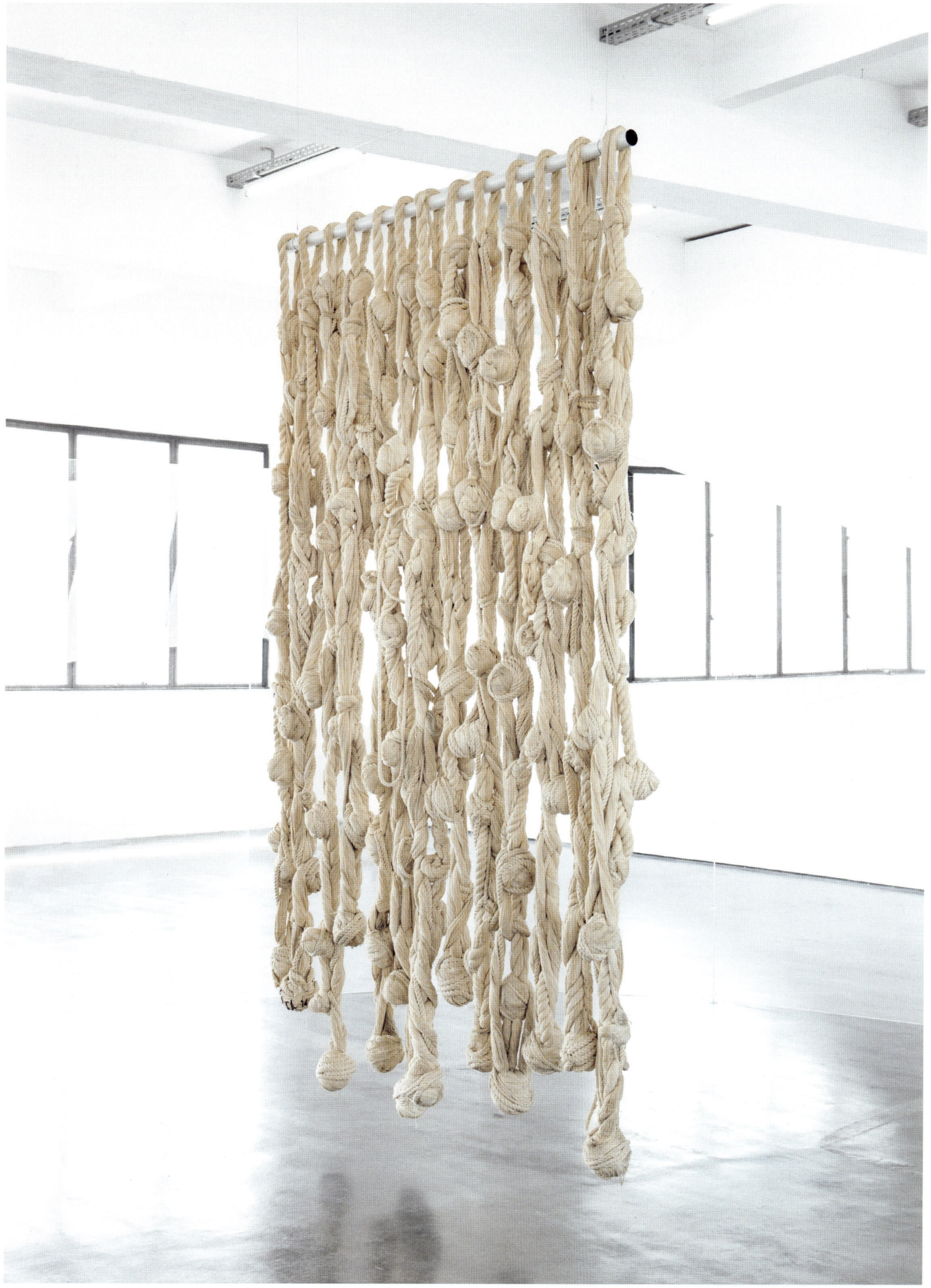

7

8

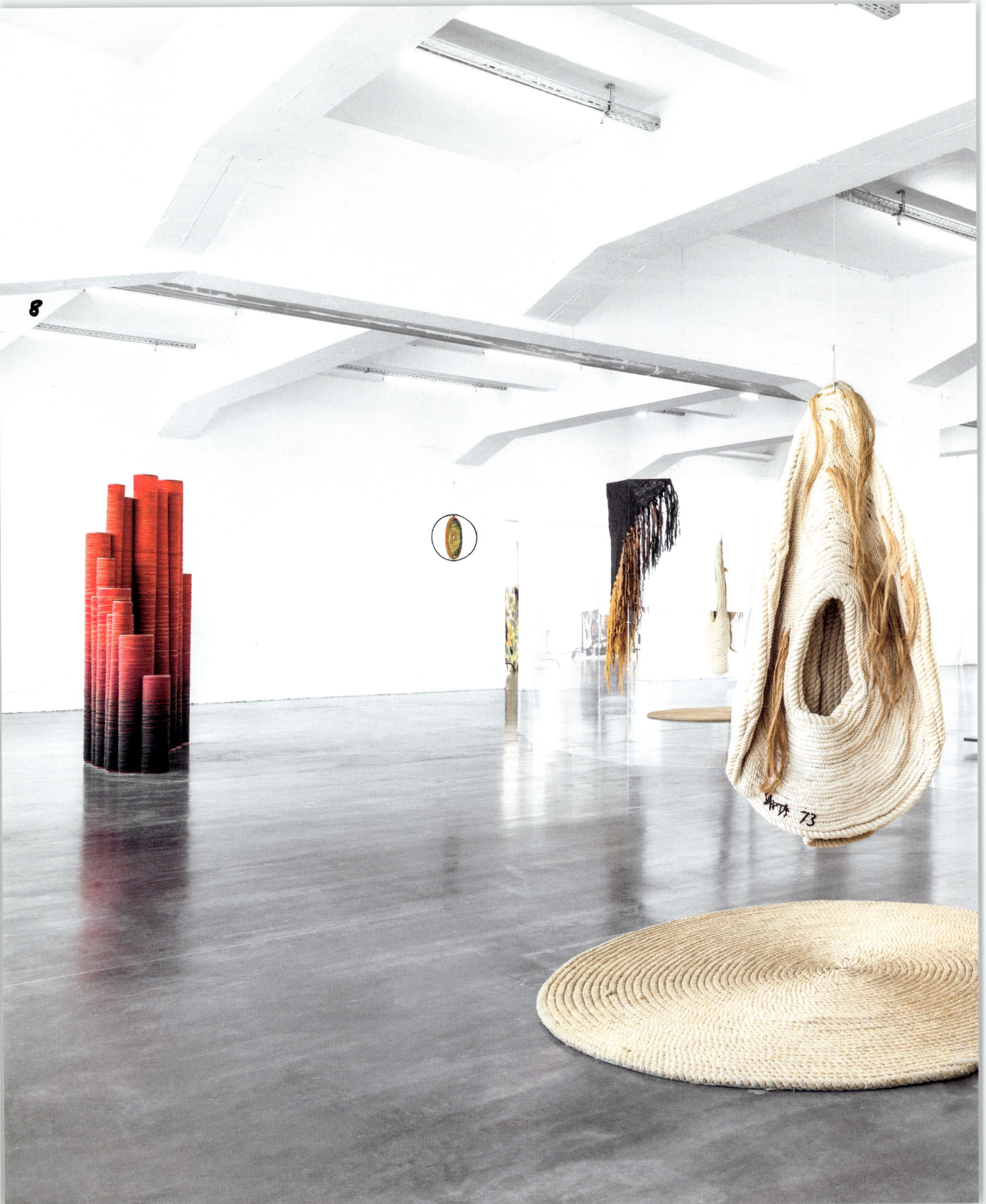

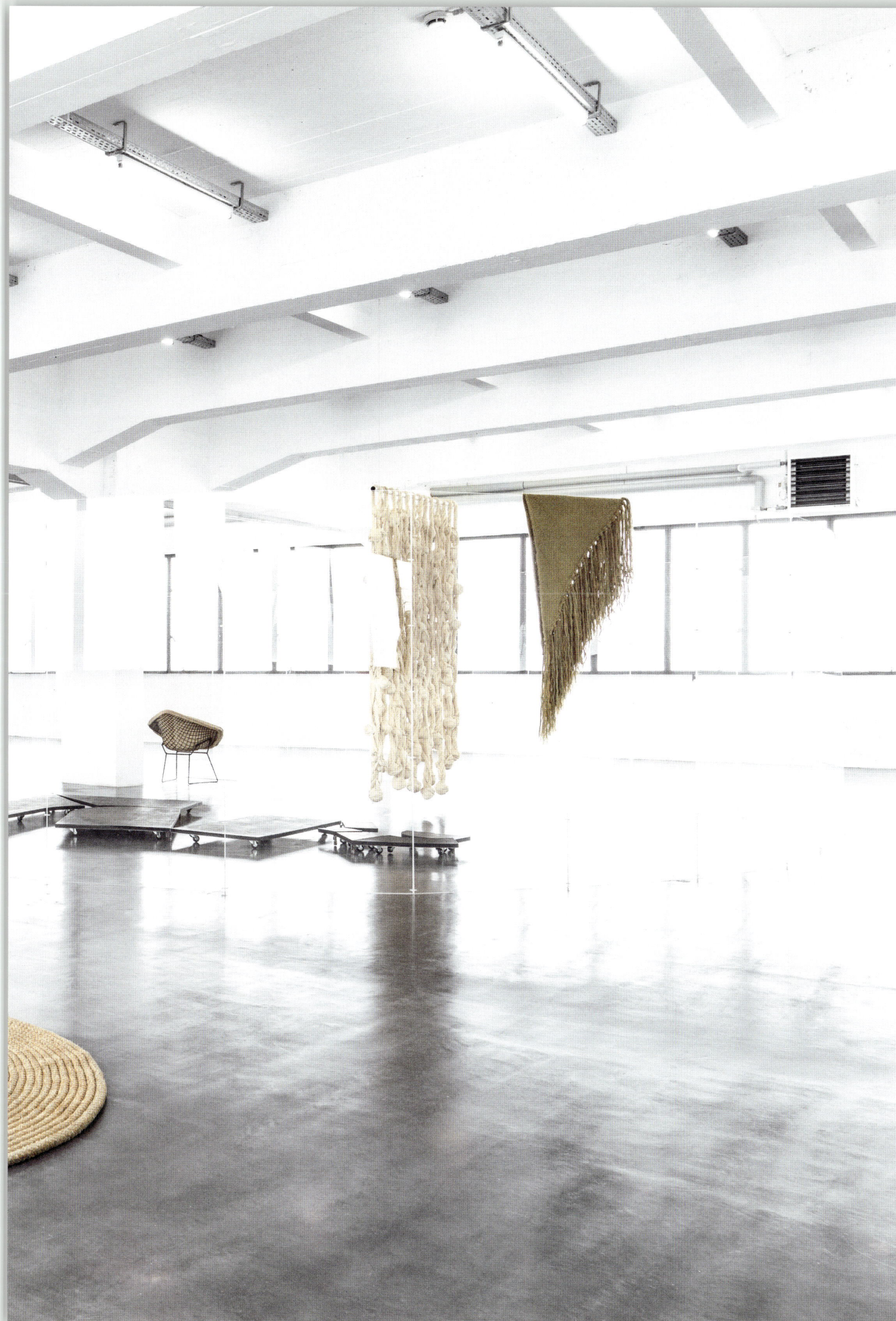

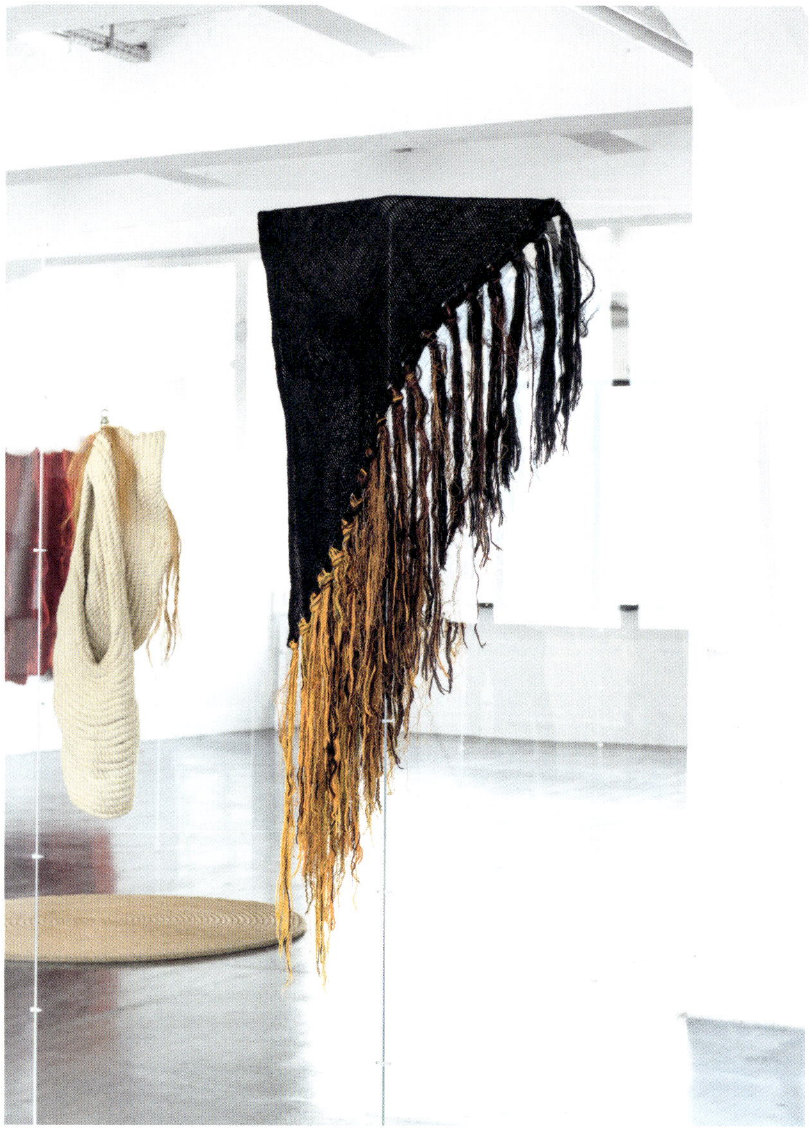

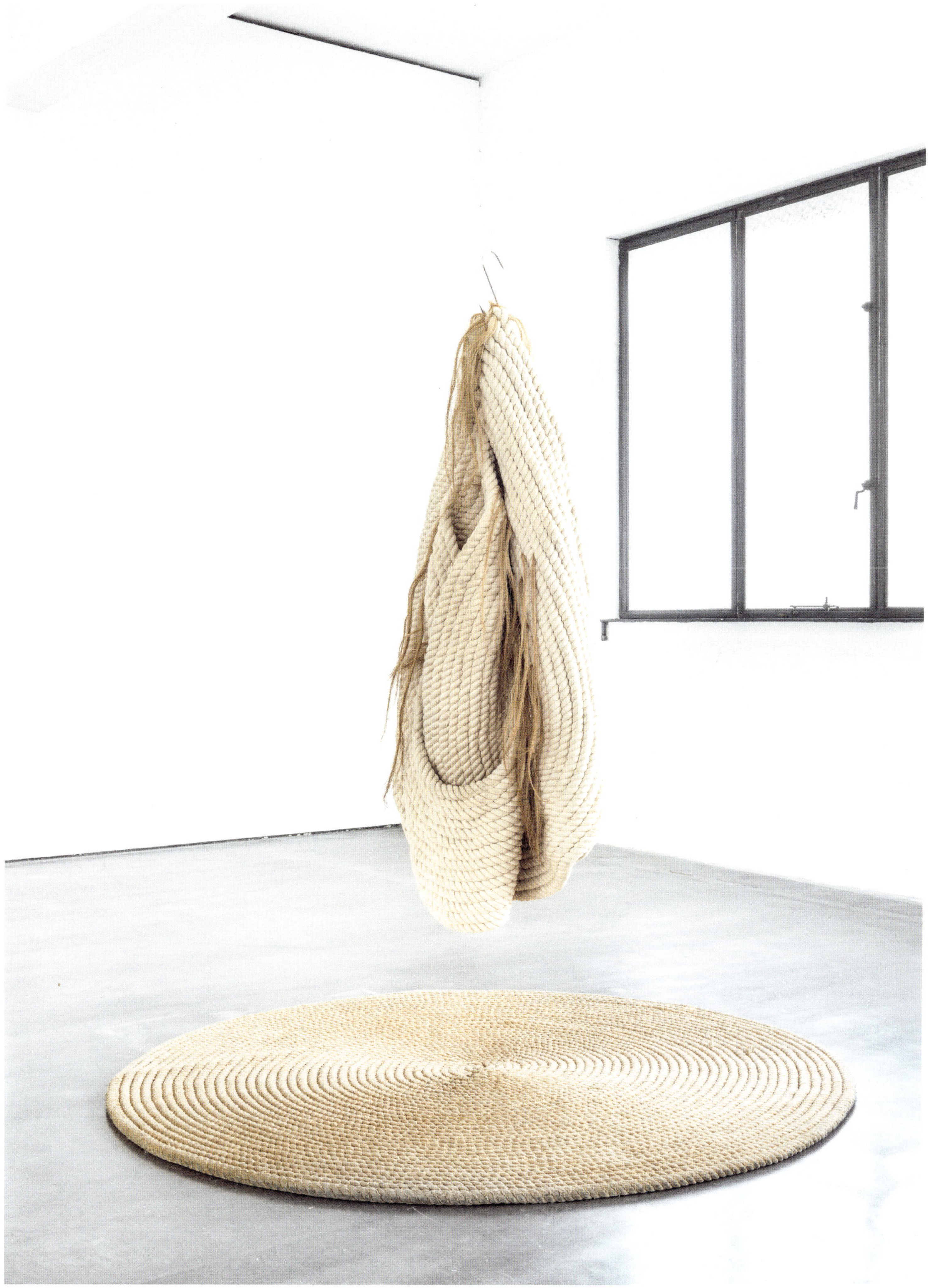

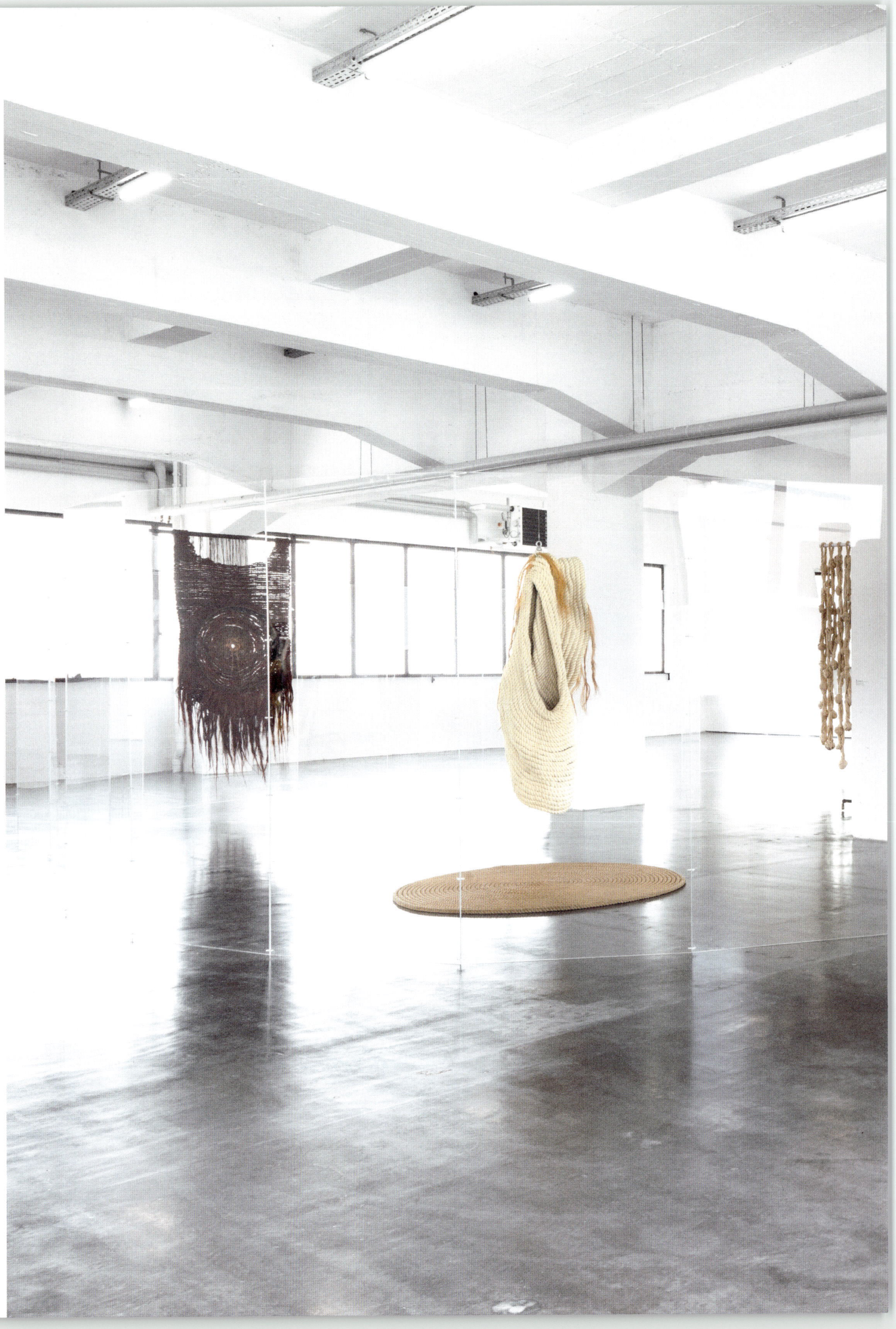

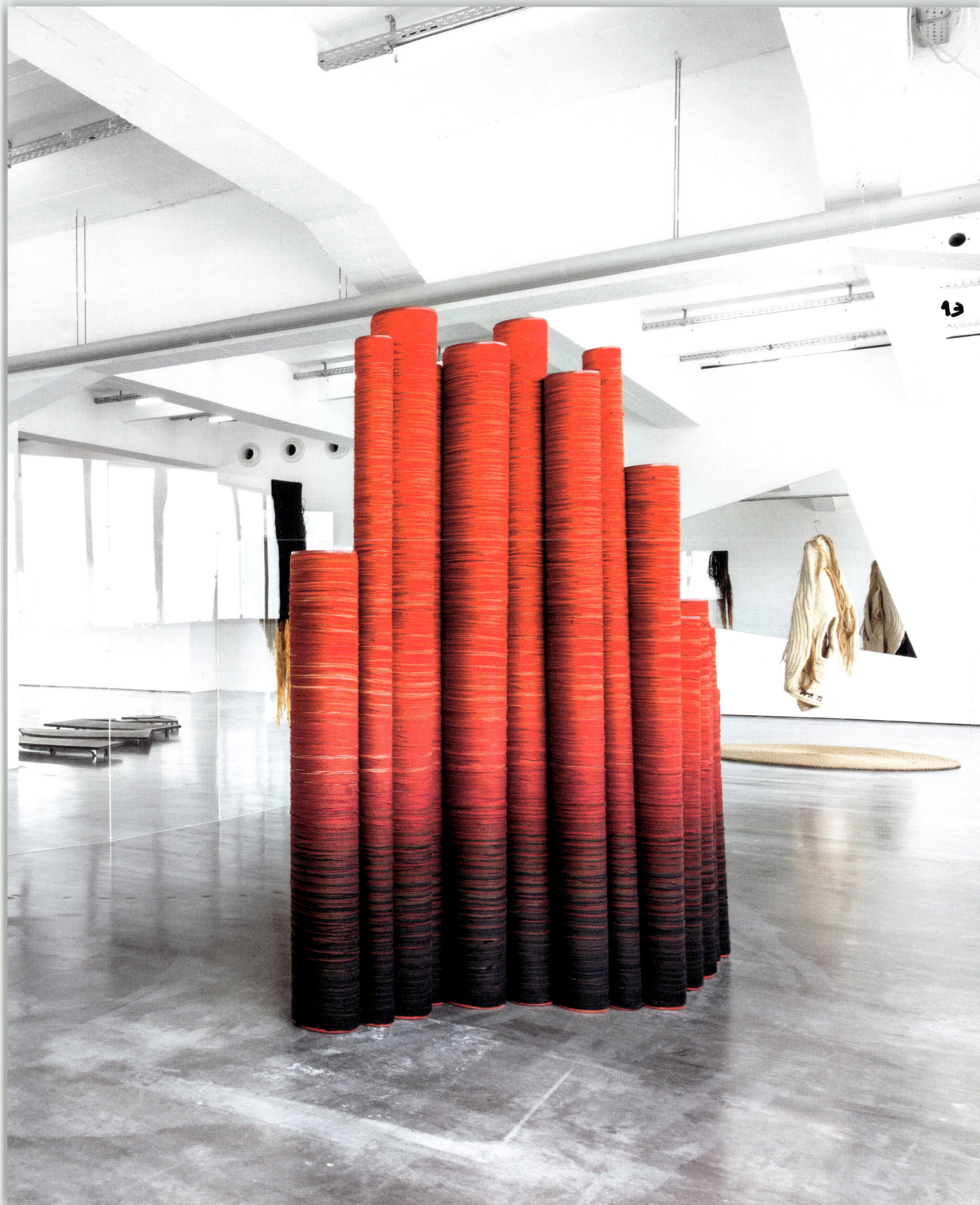

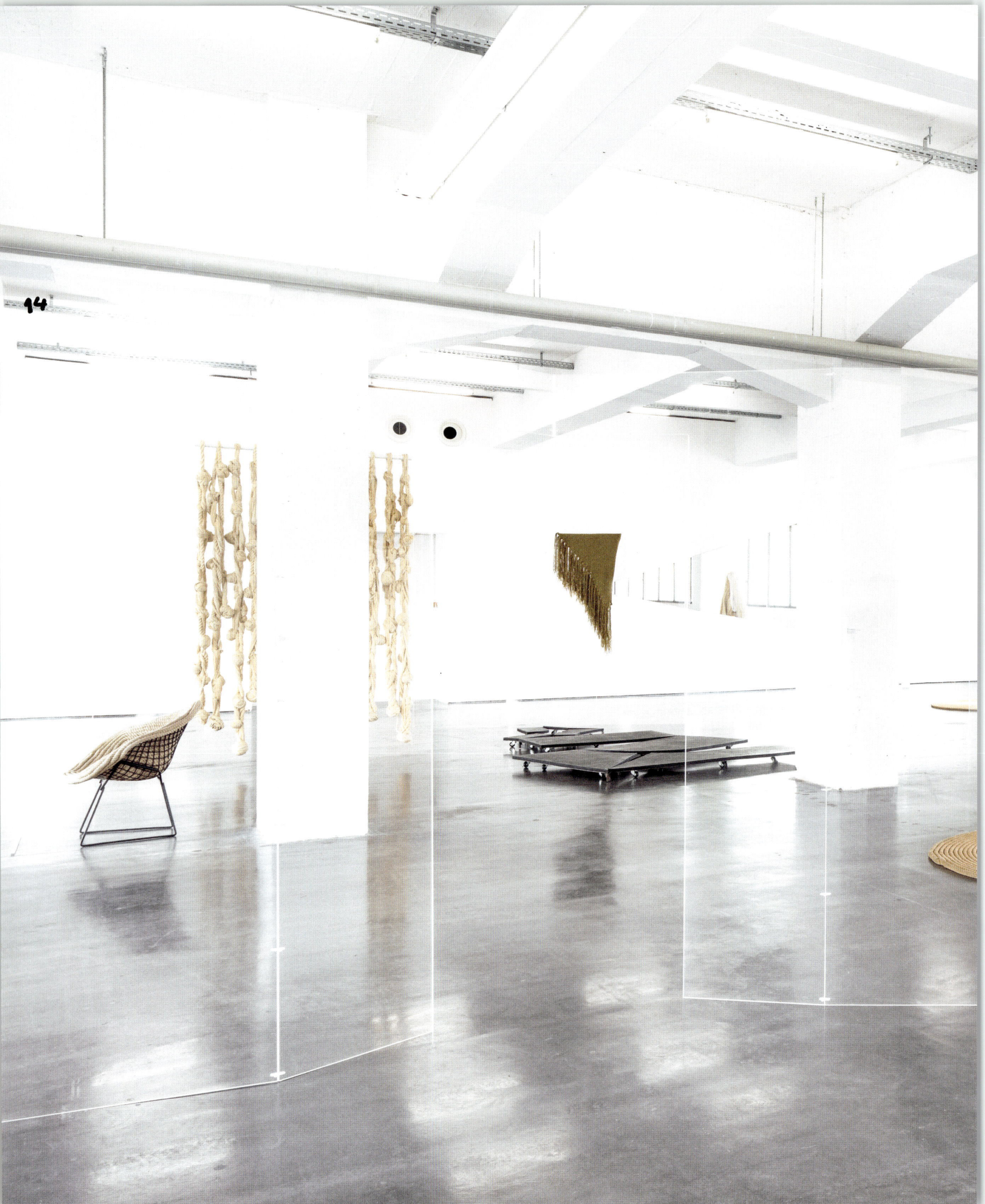

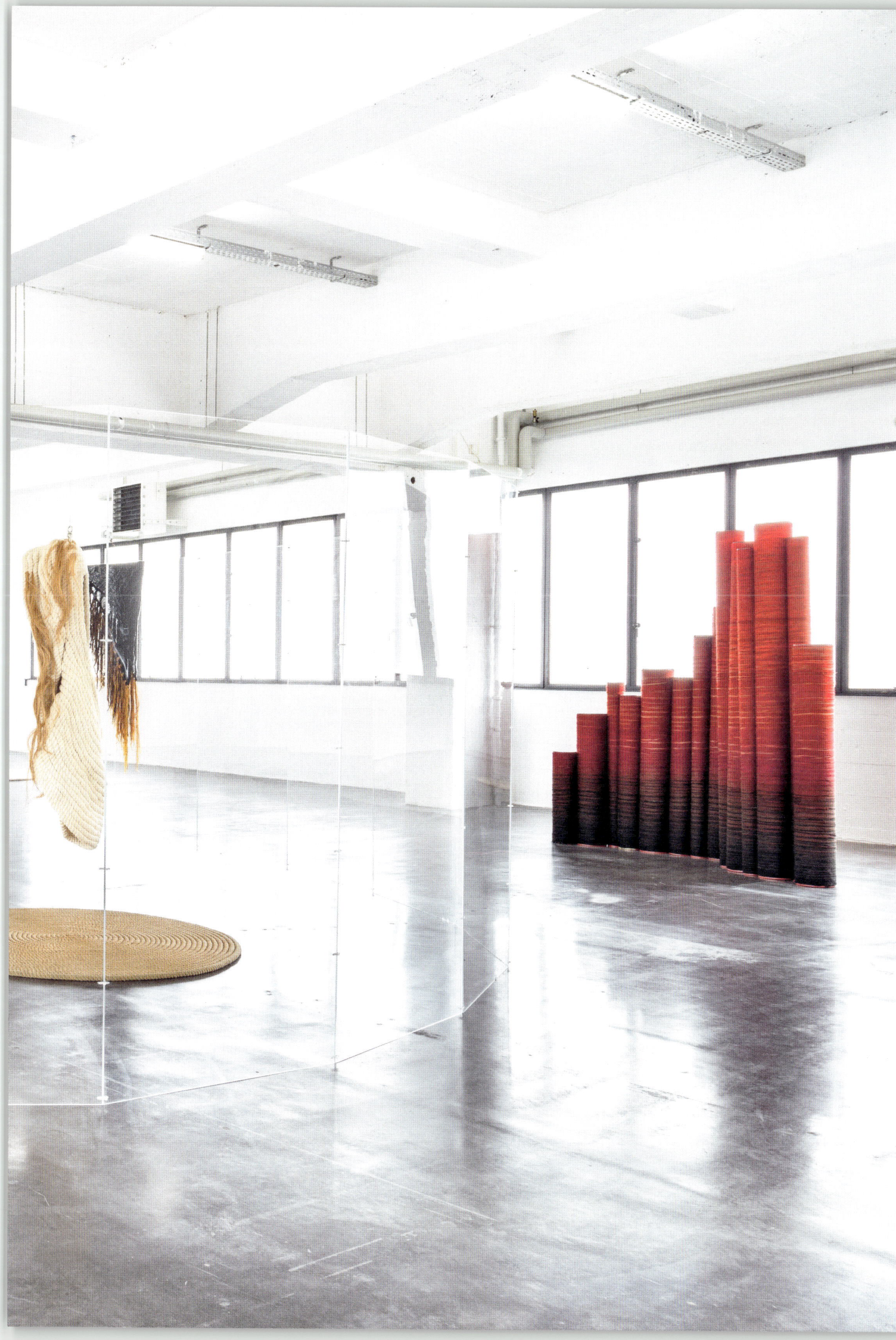

15

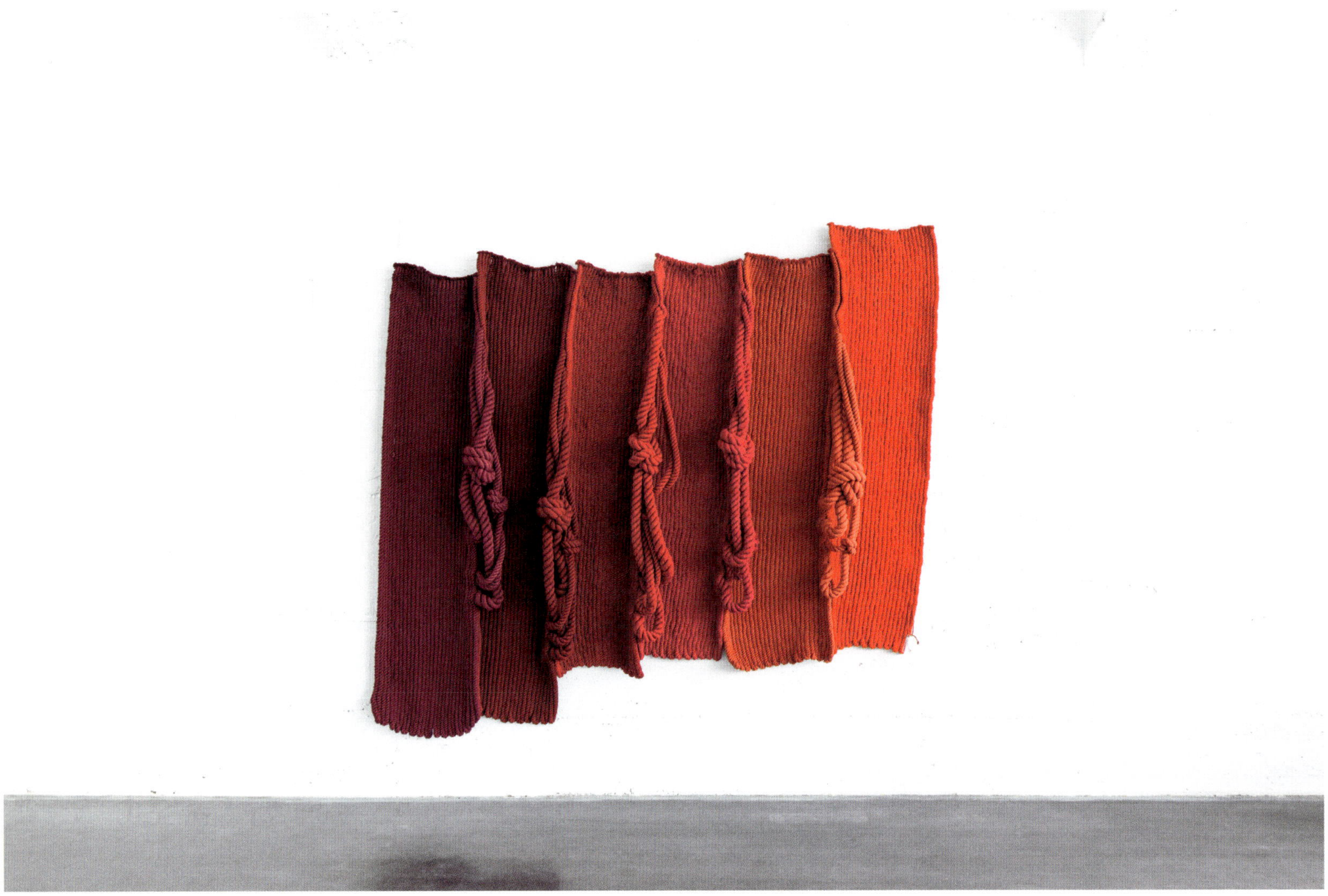

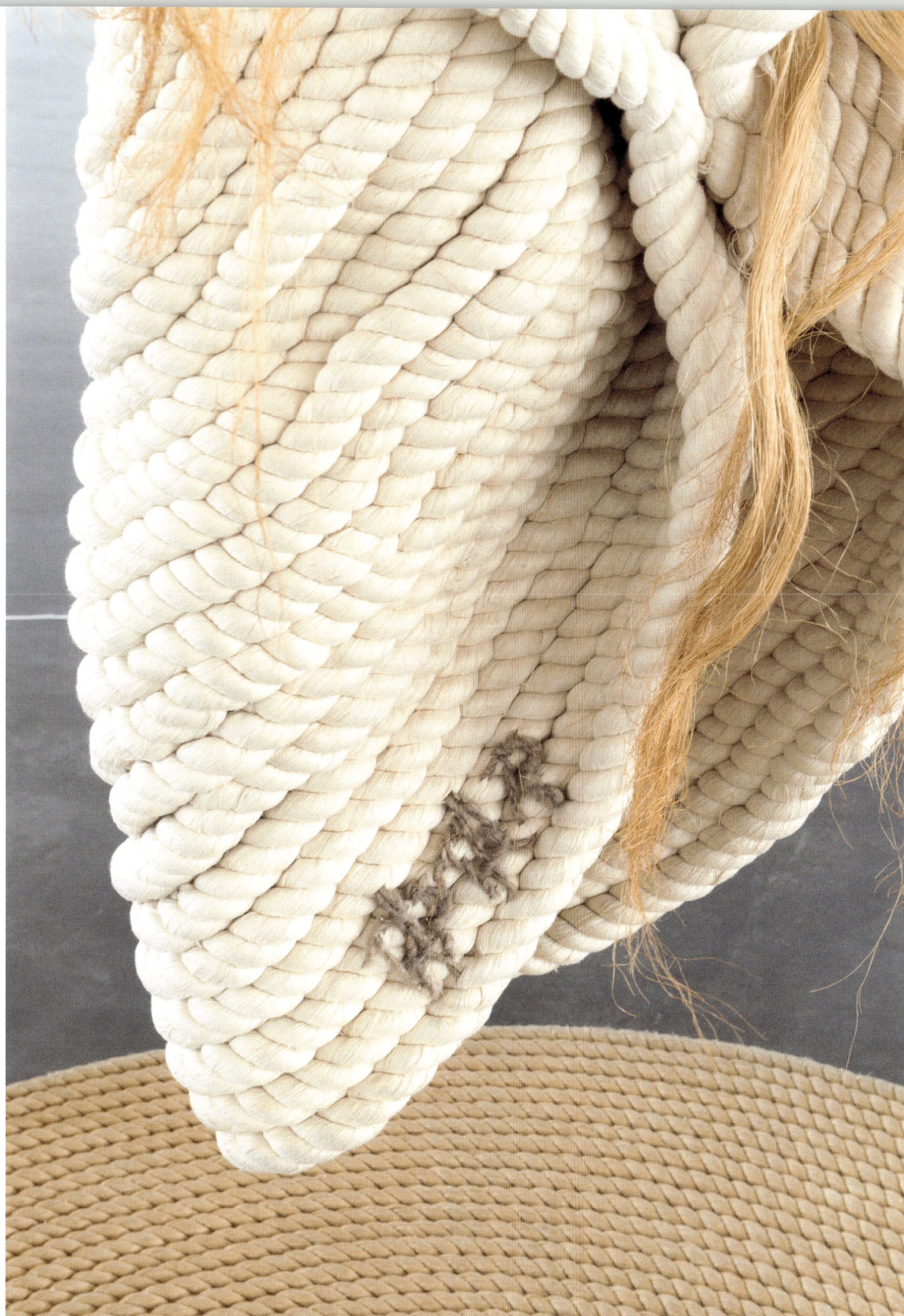

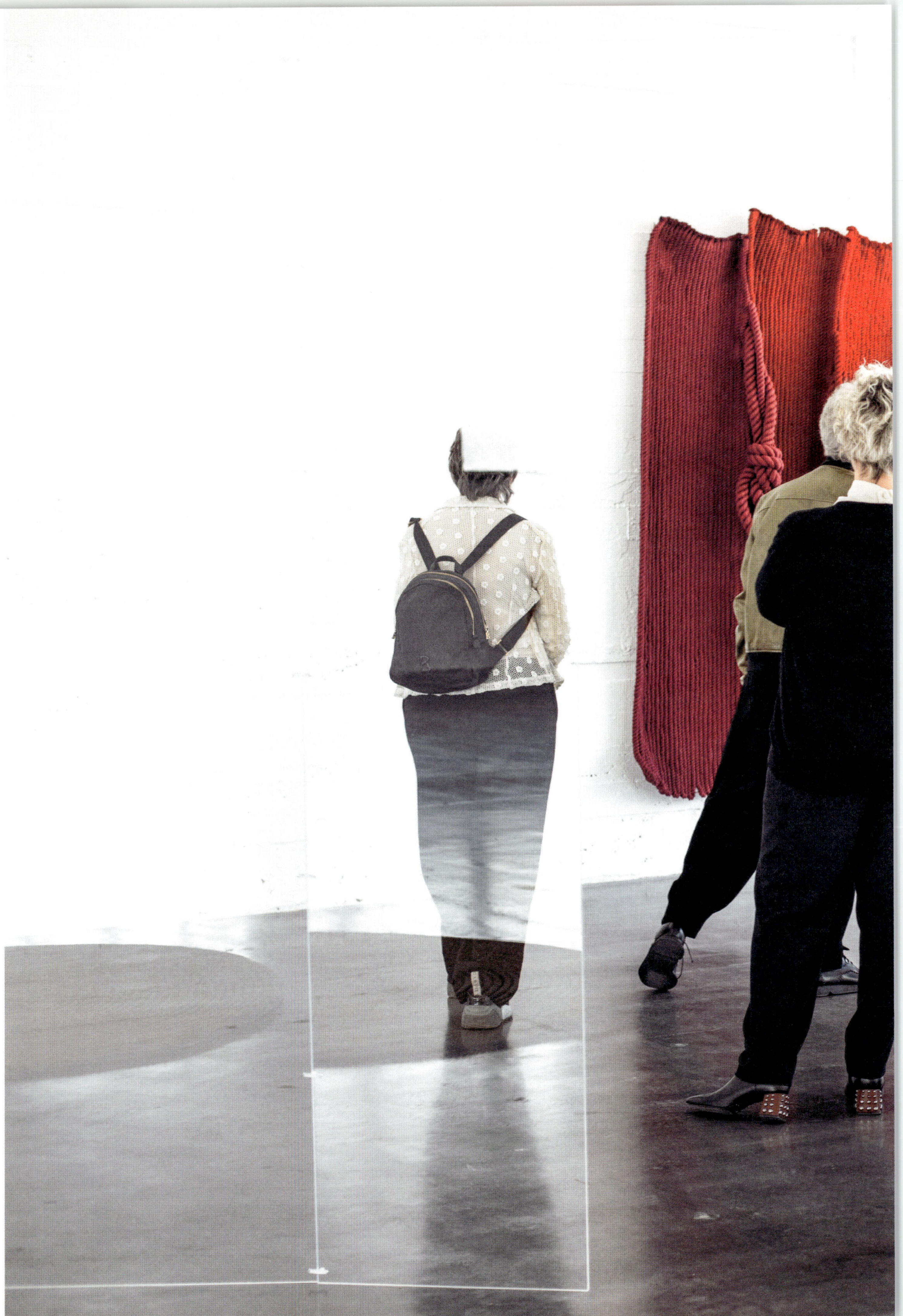

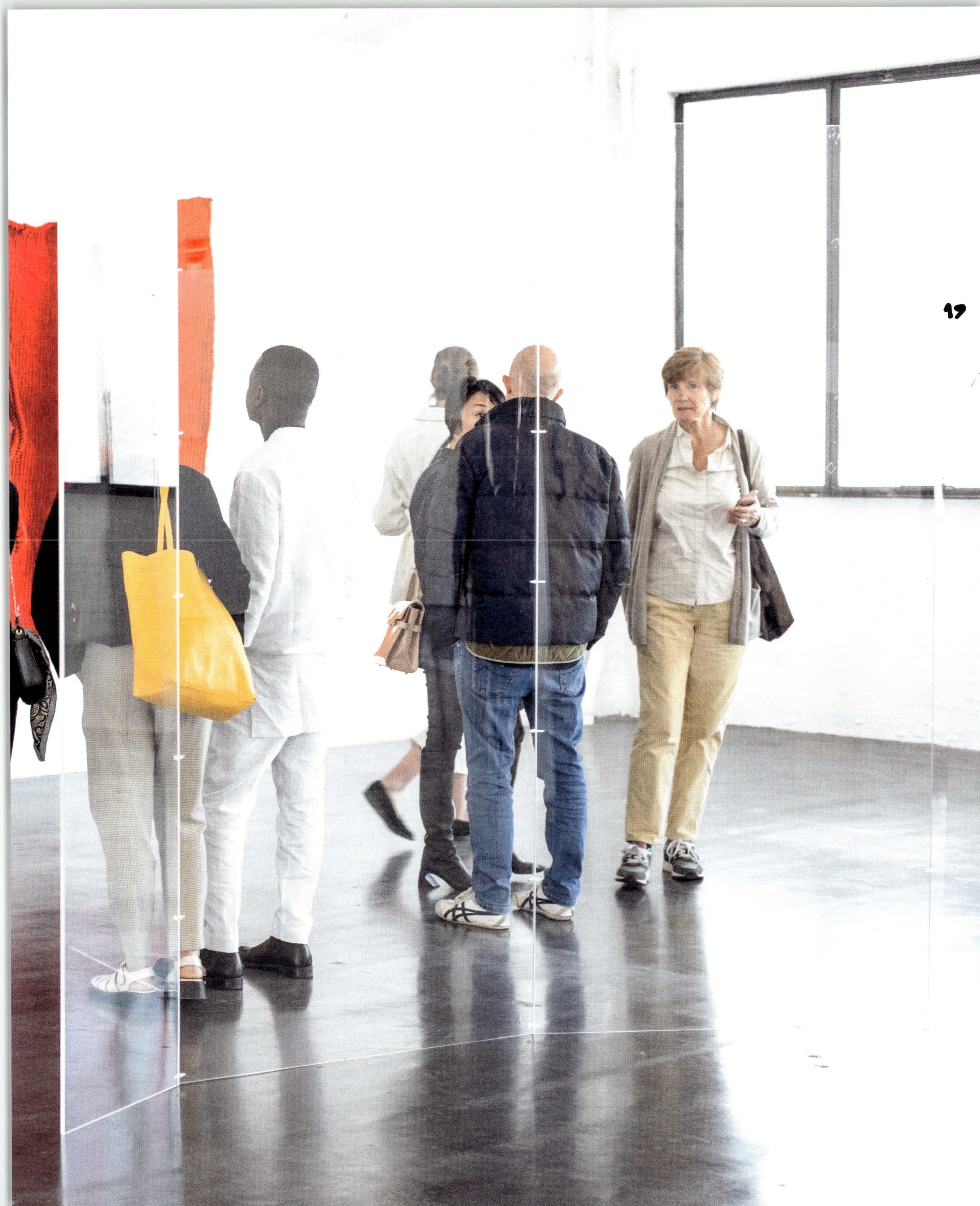

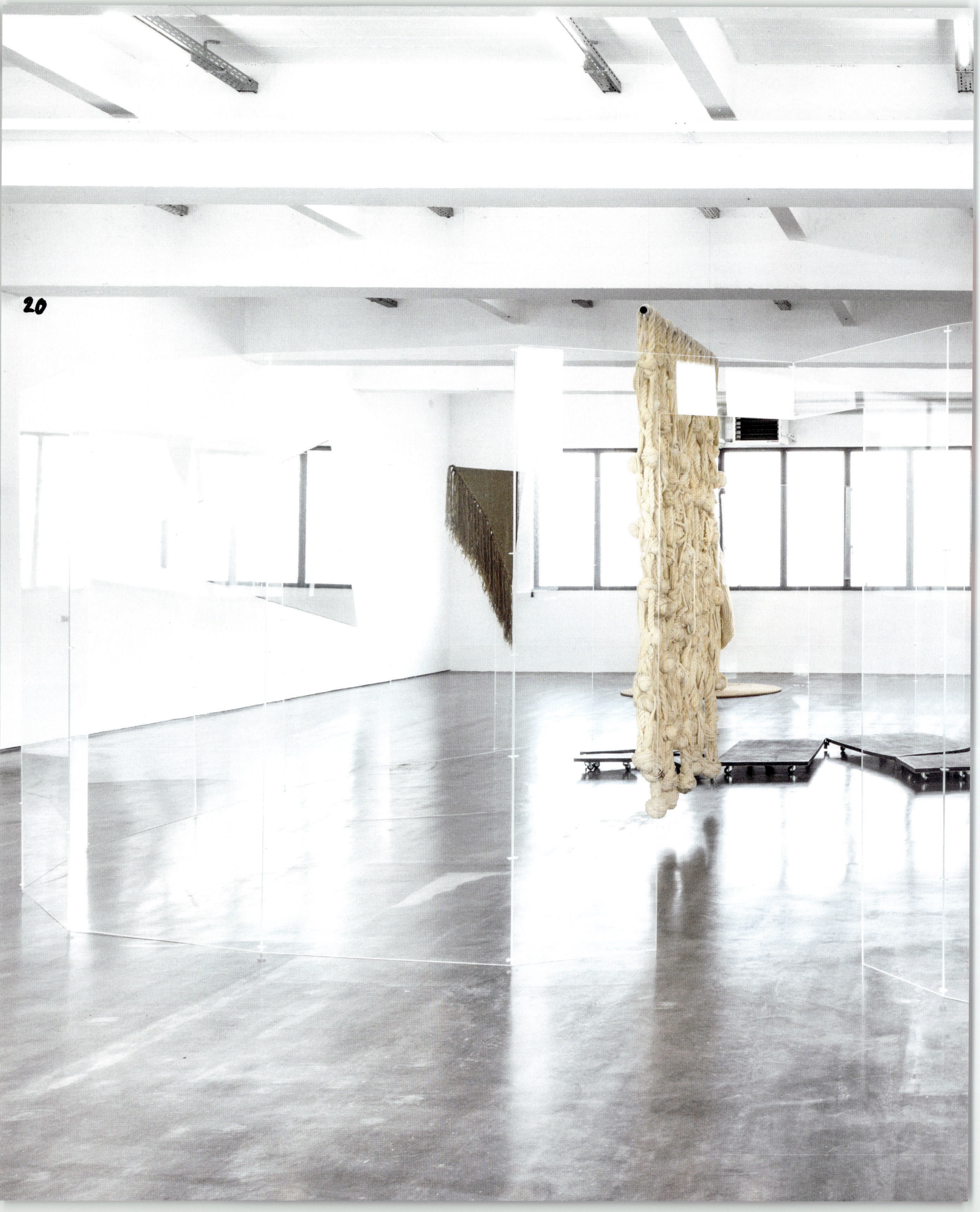

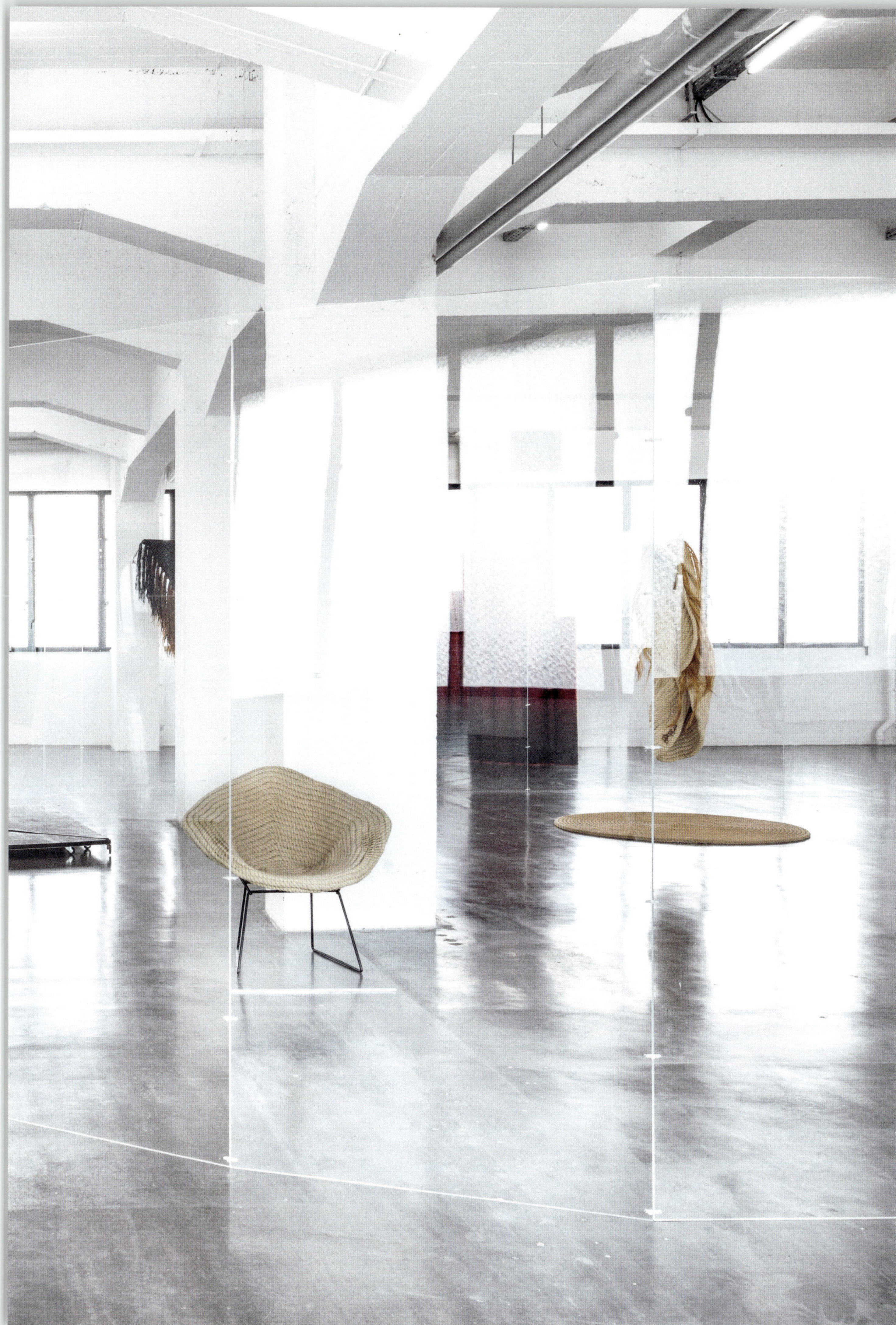

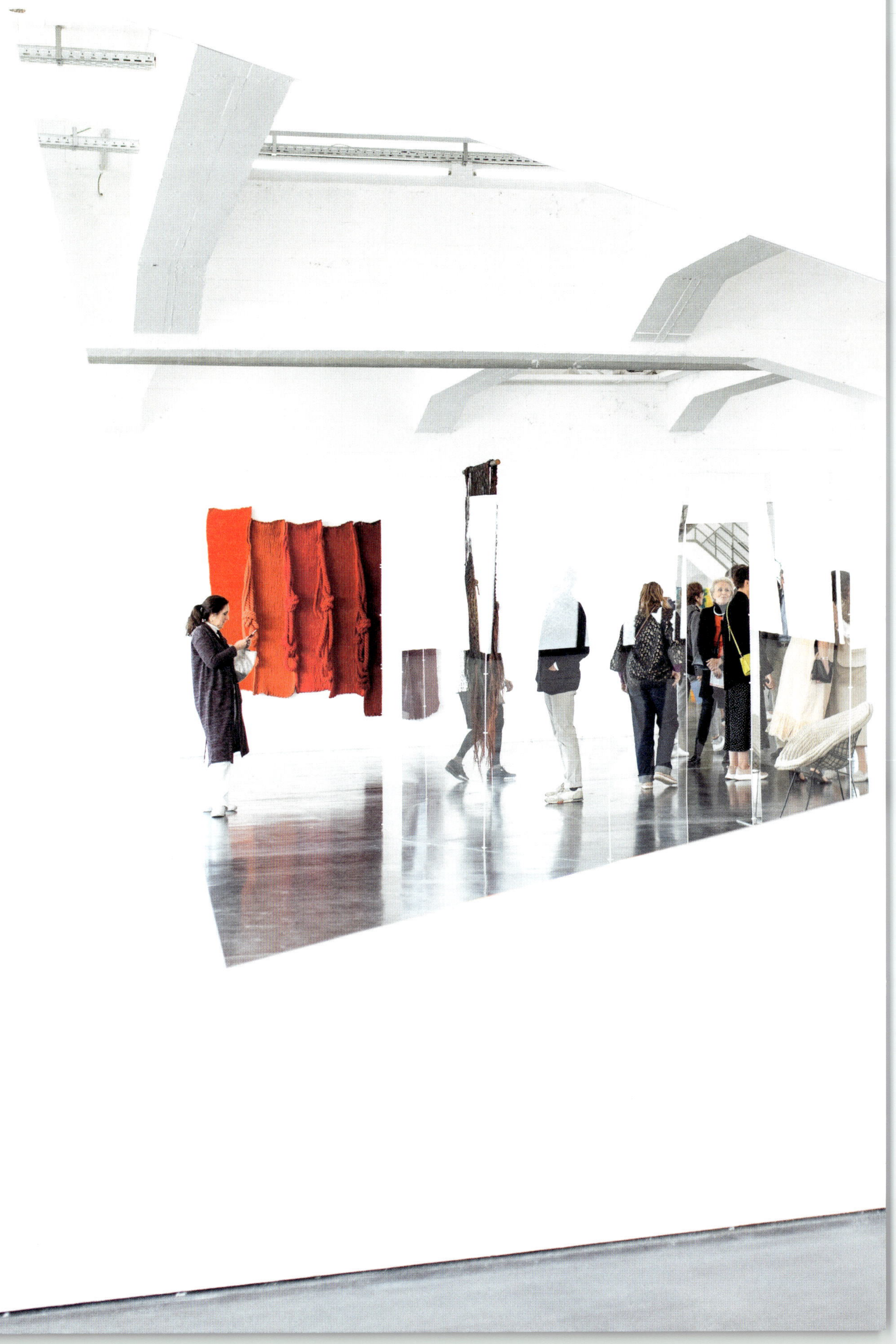

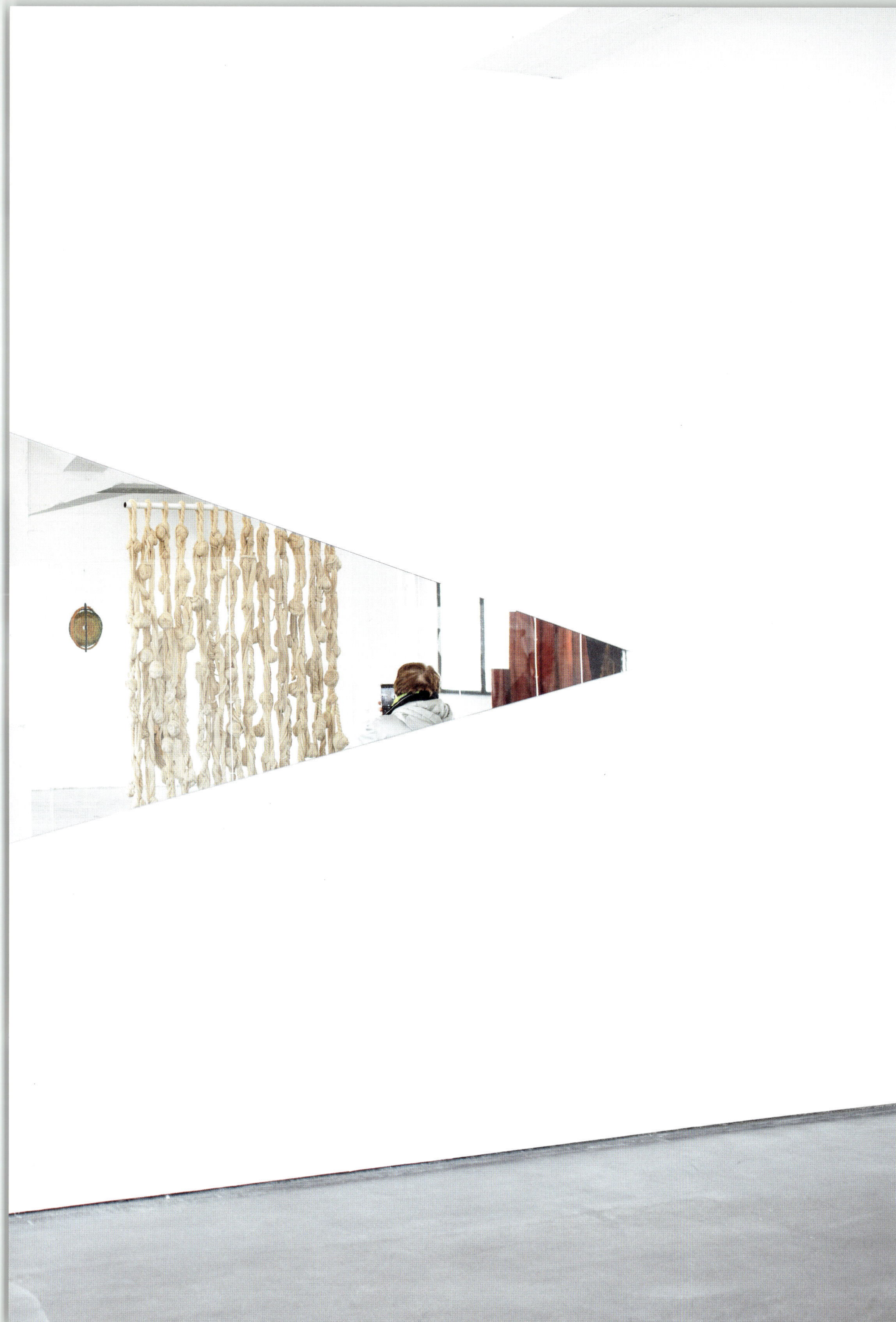

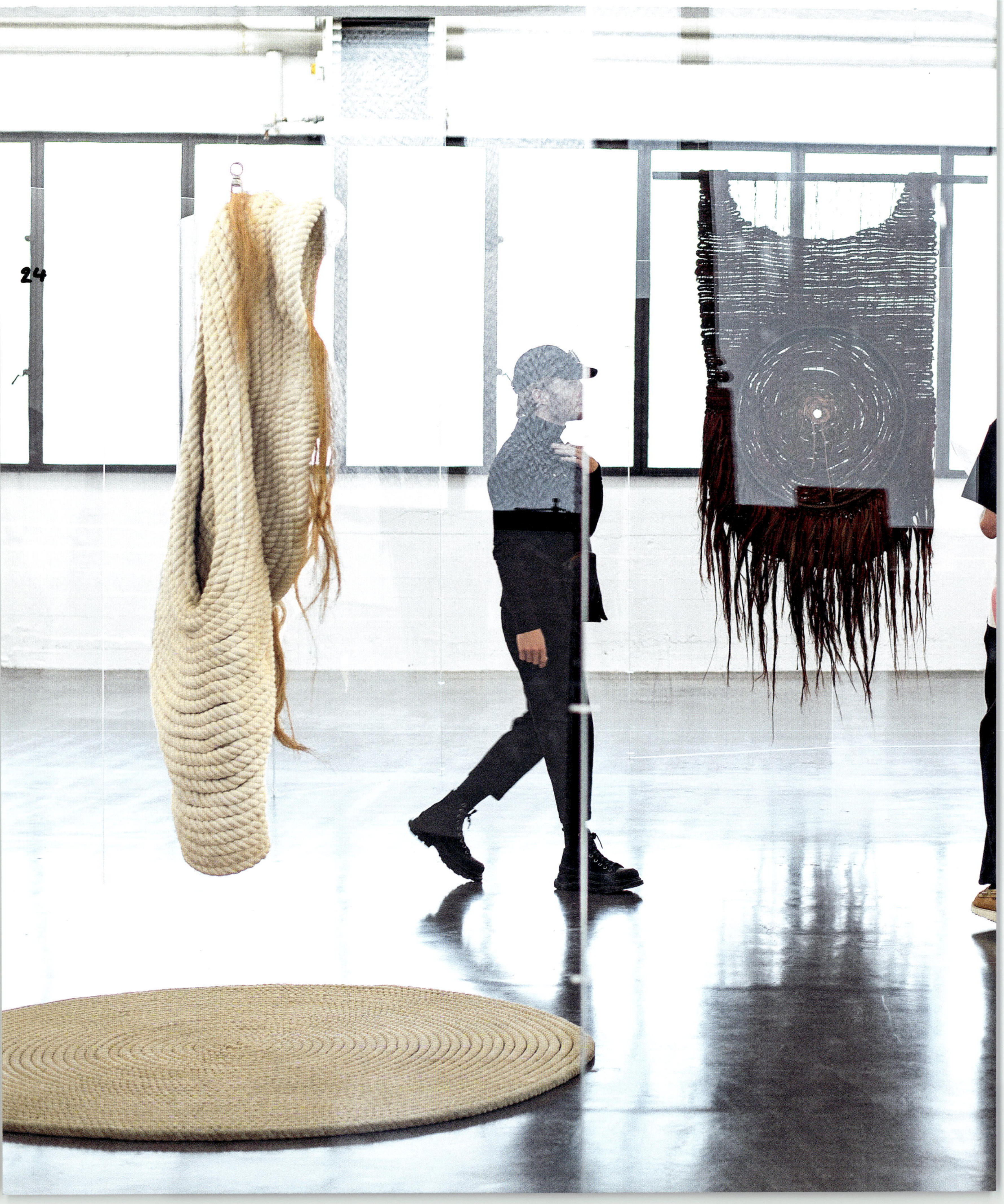

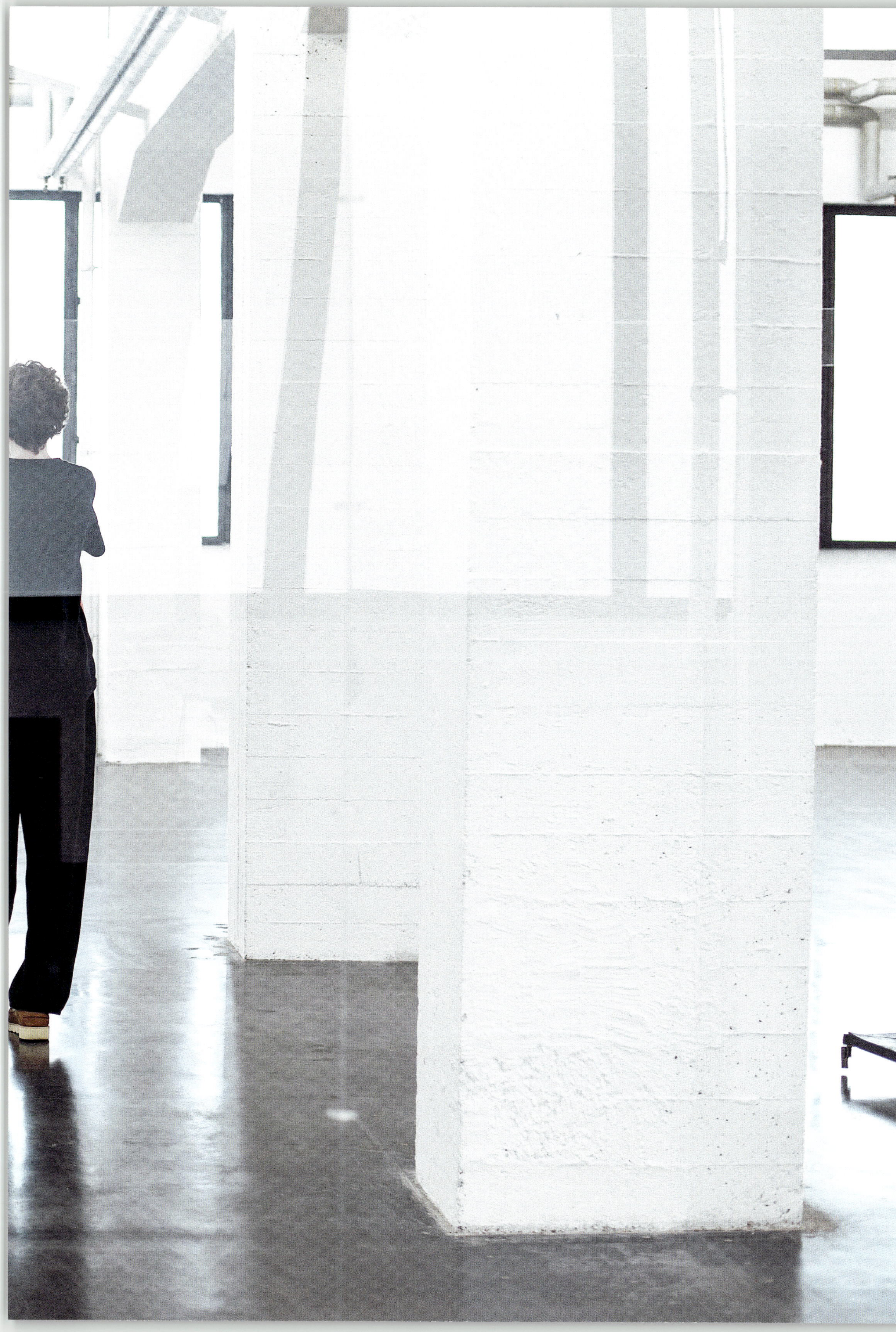

26

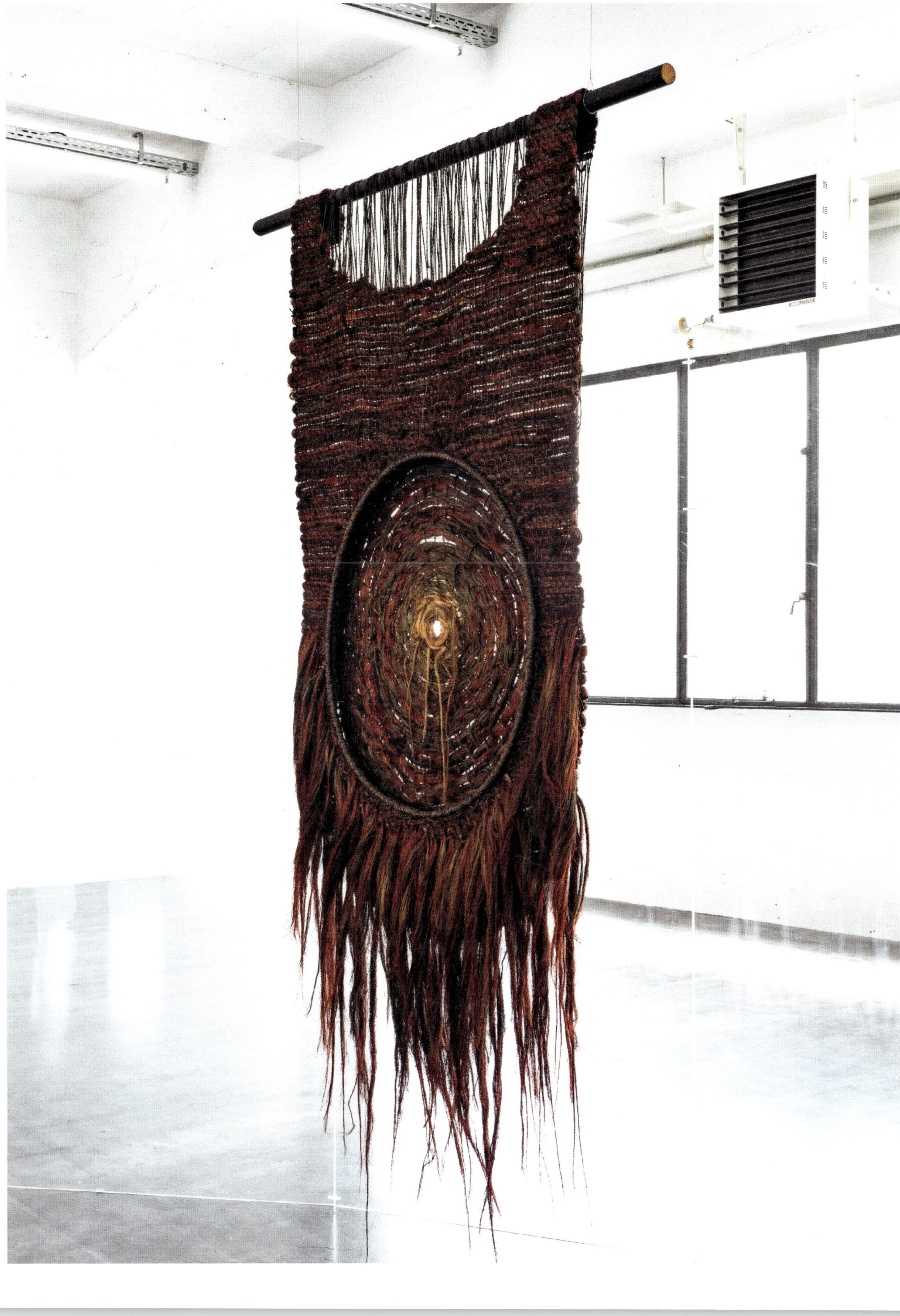

28

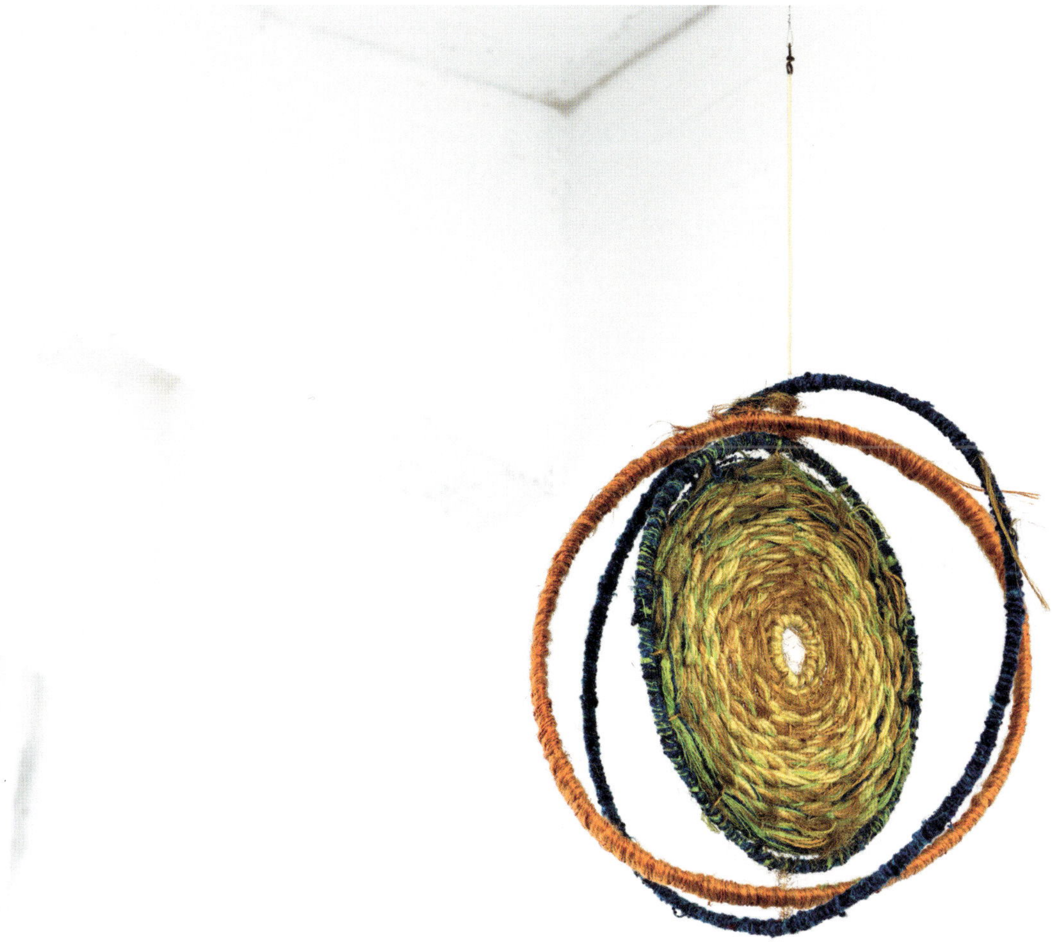

30

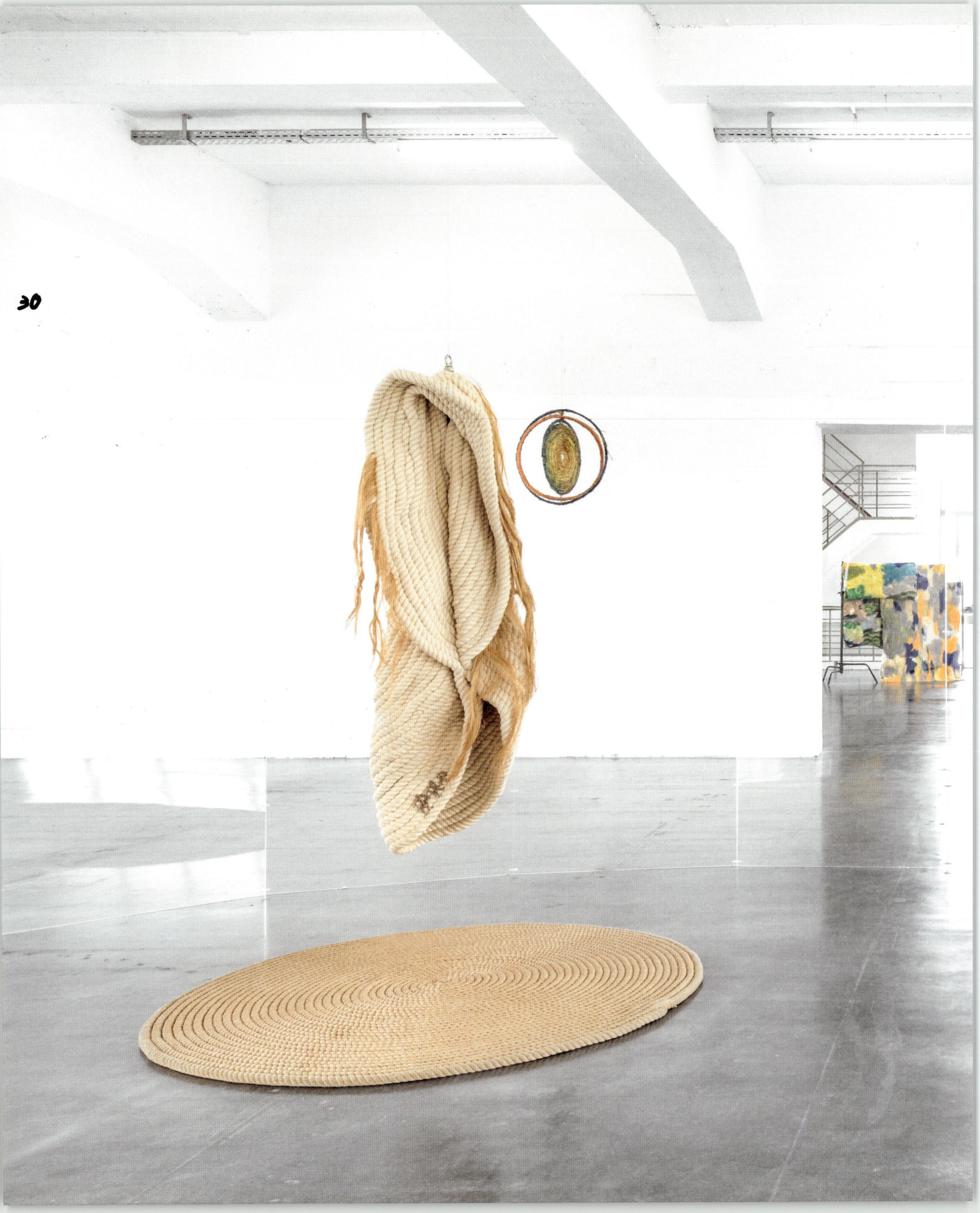

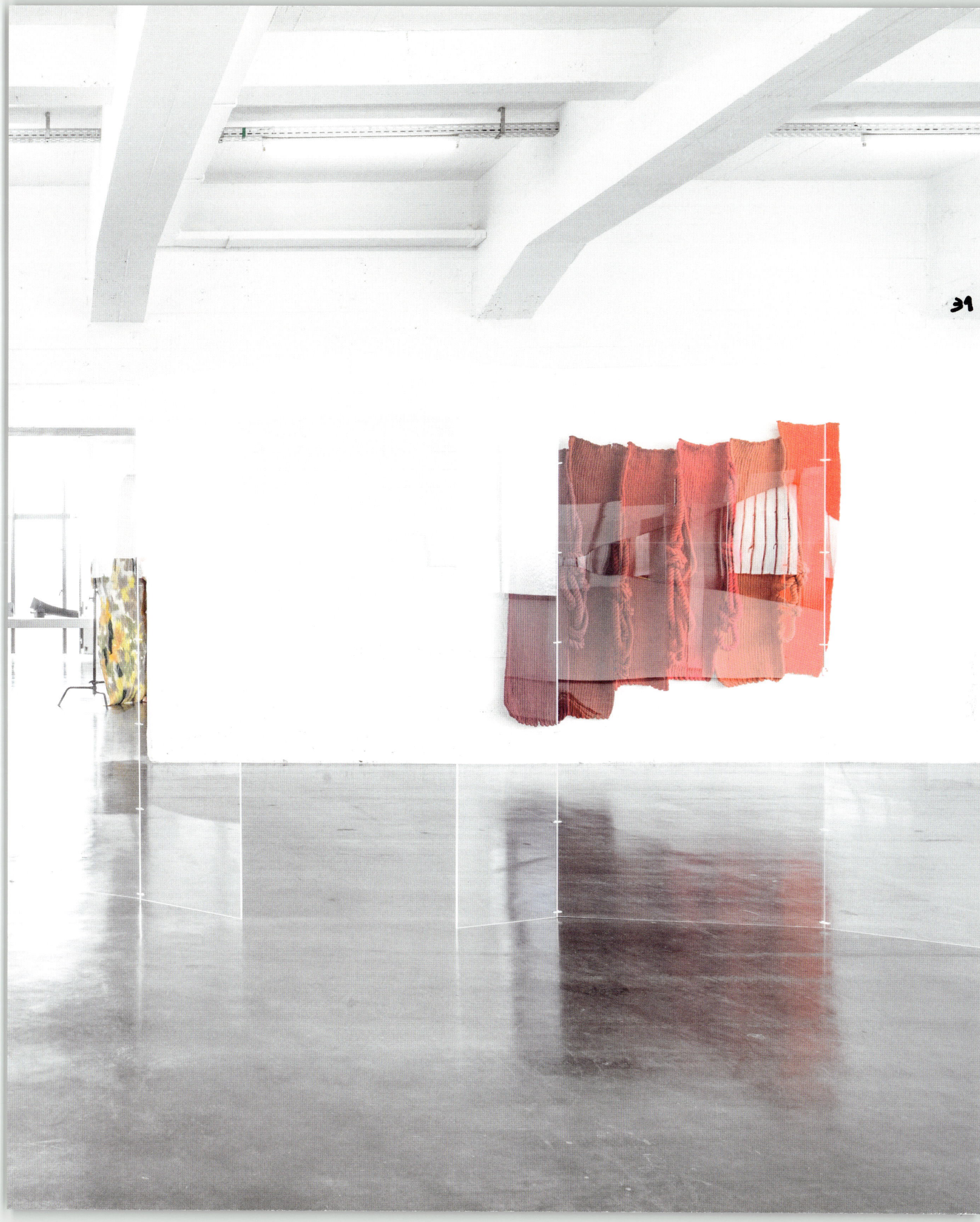

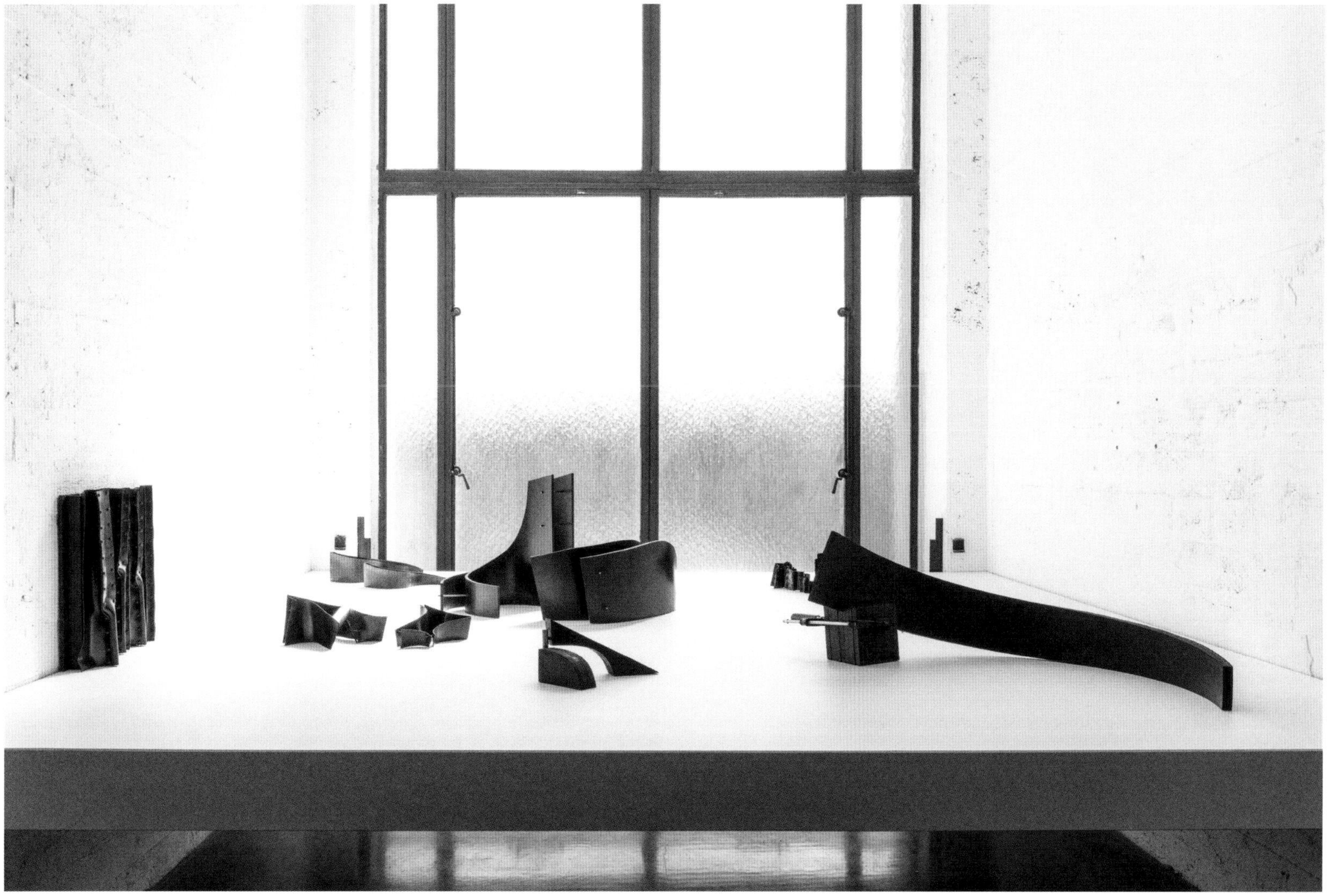

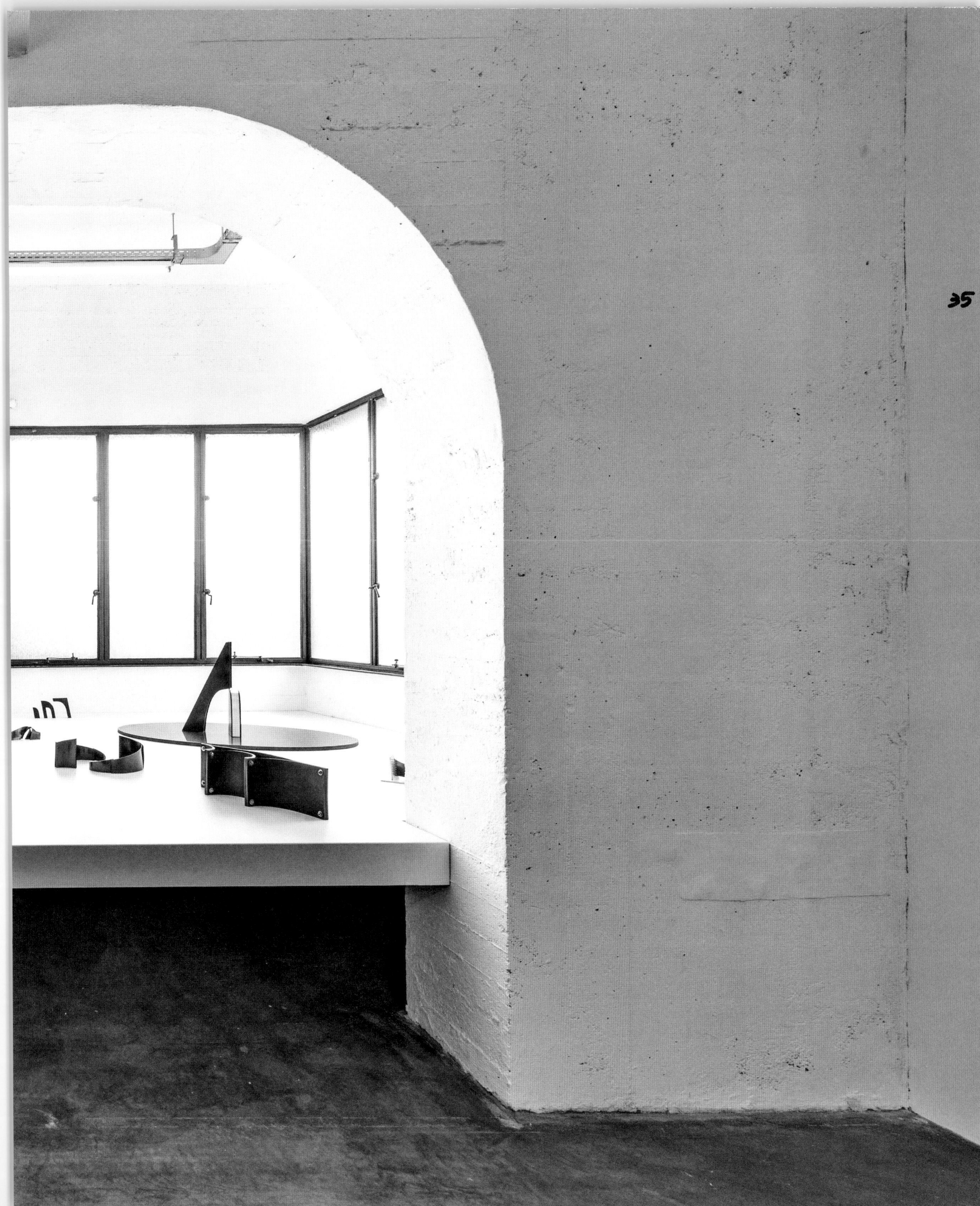

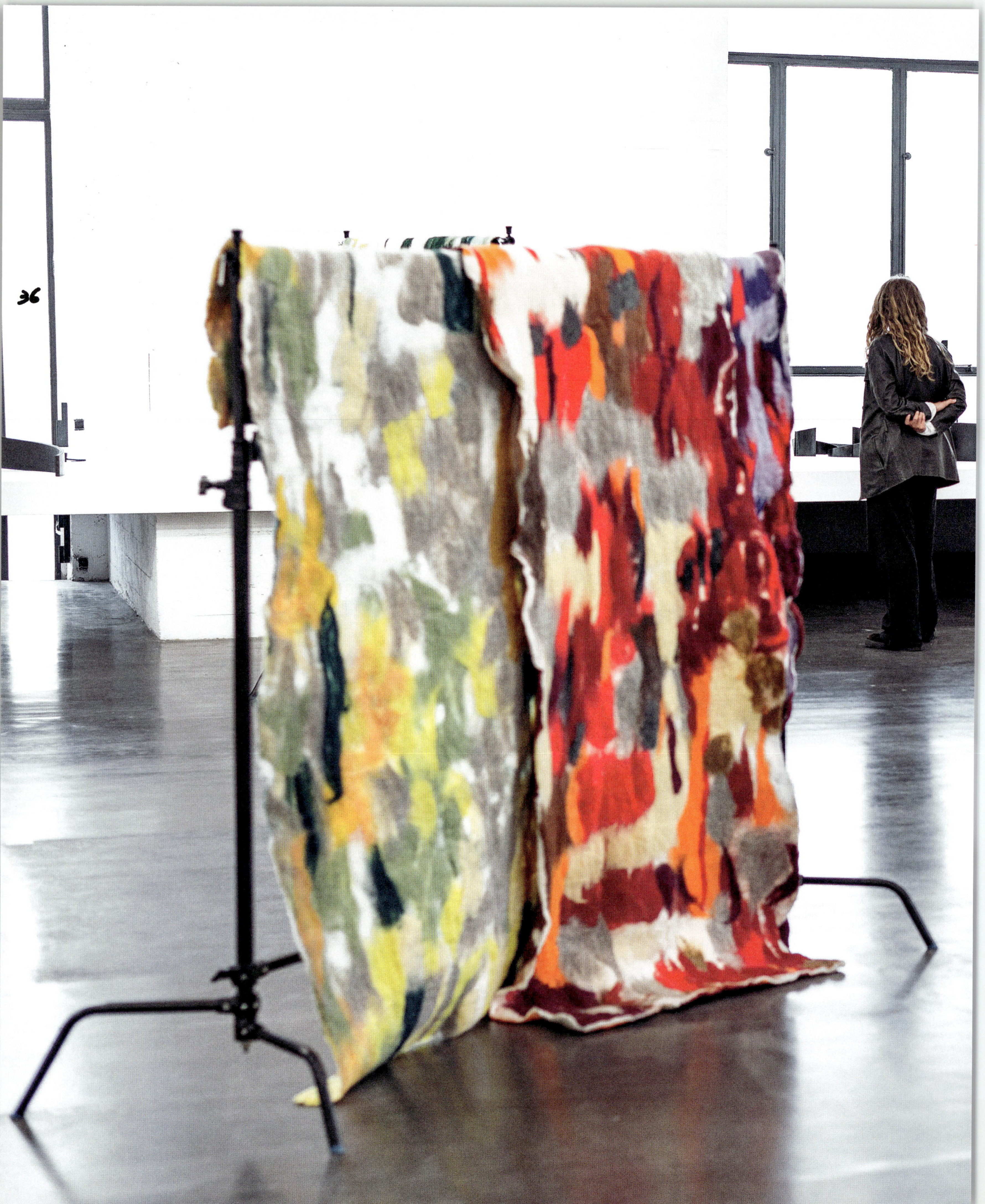

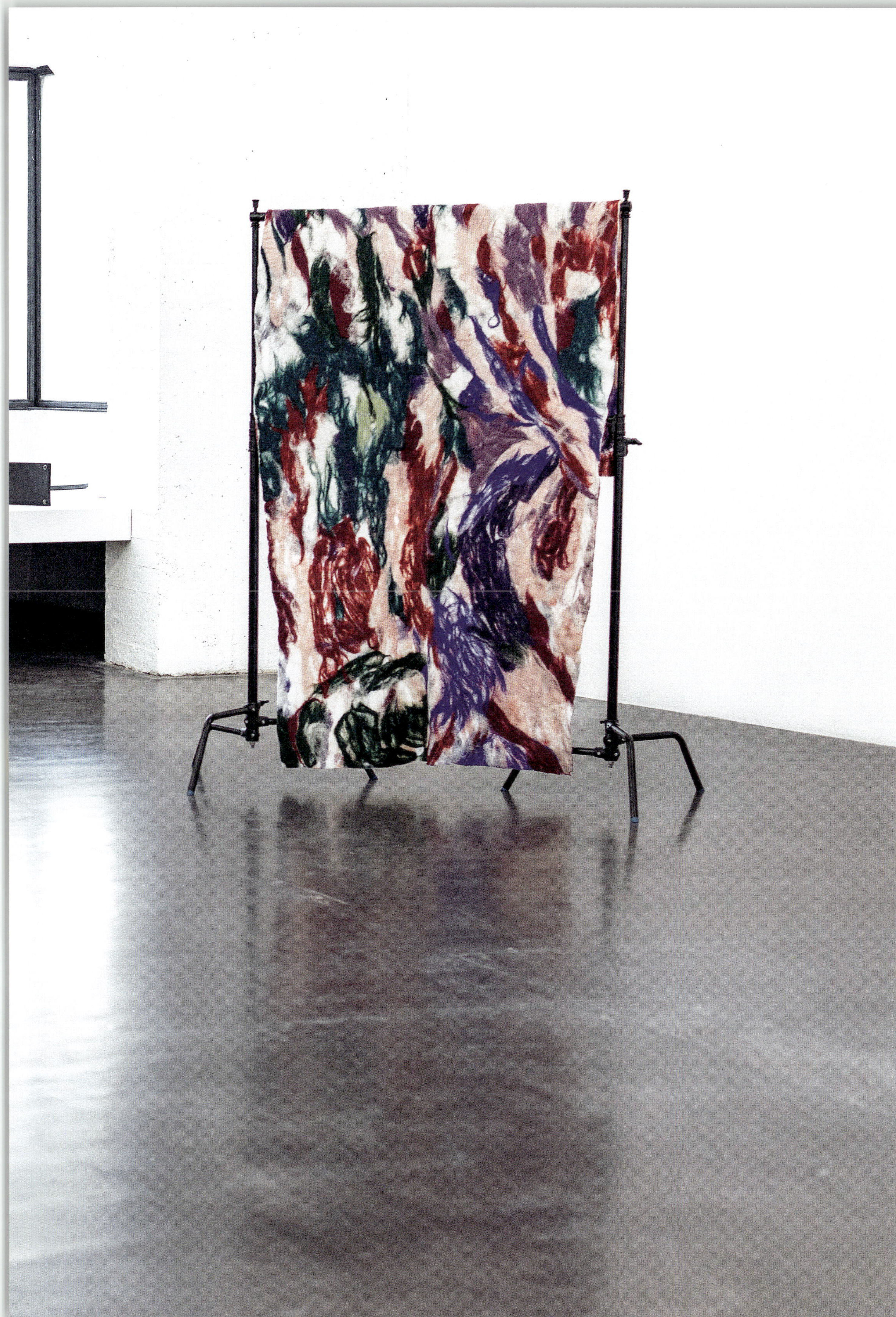

37

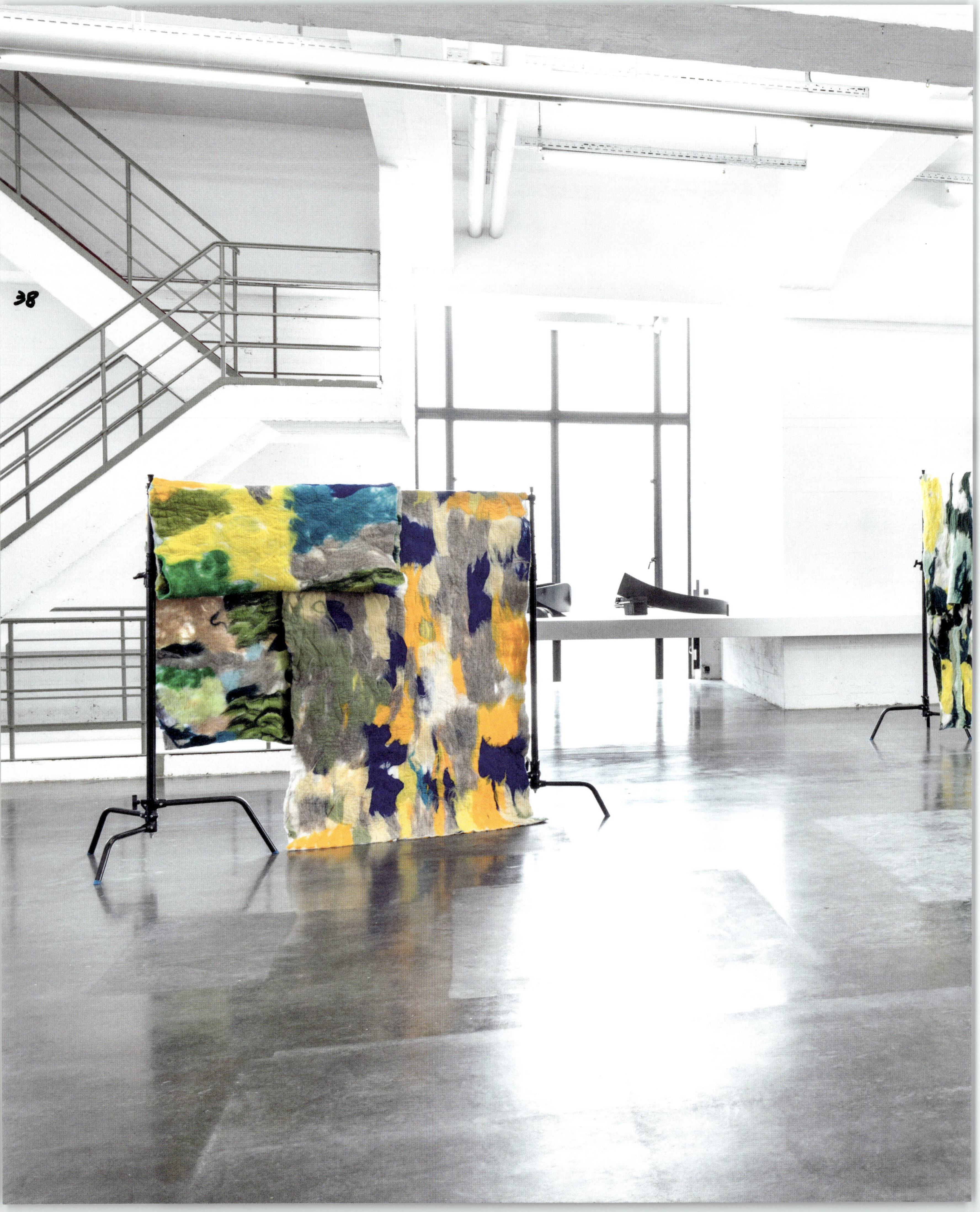
38

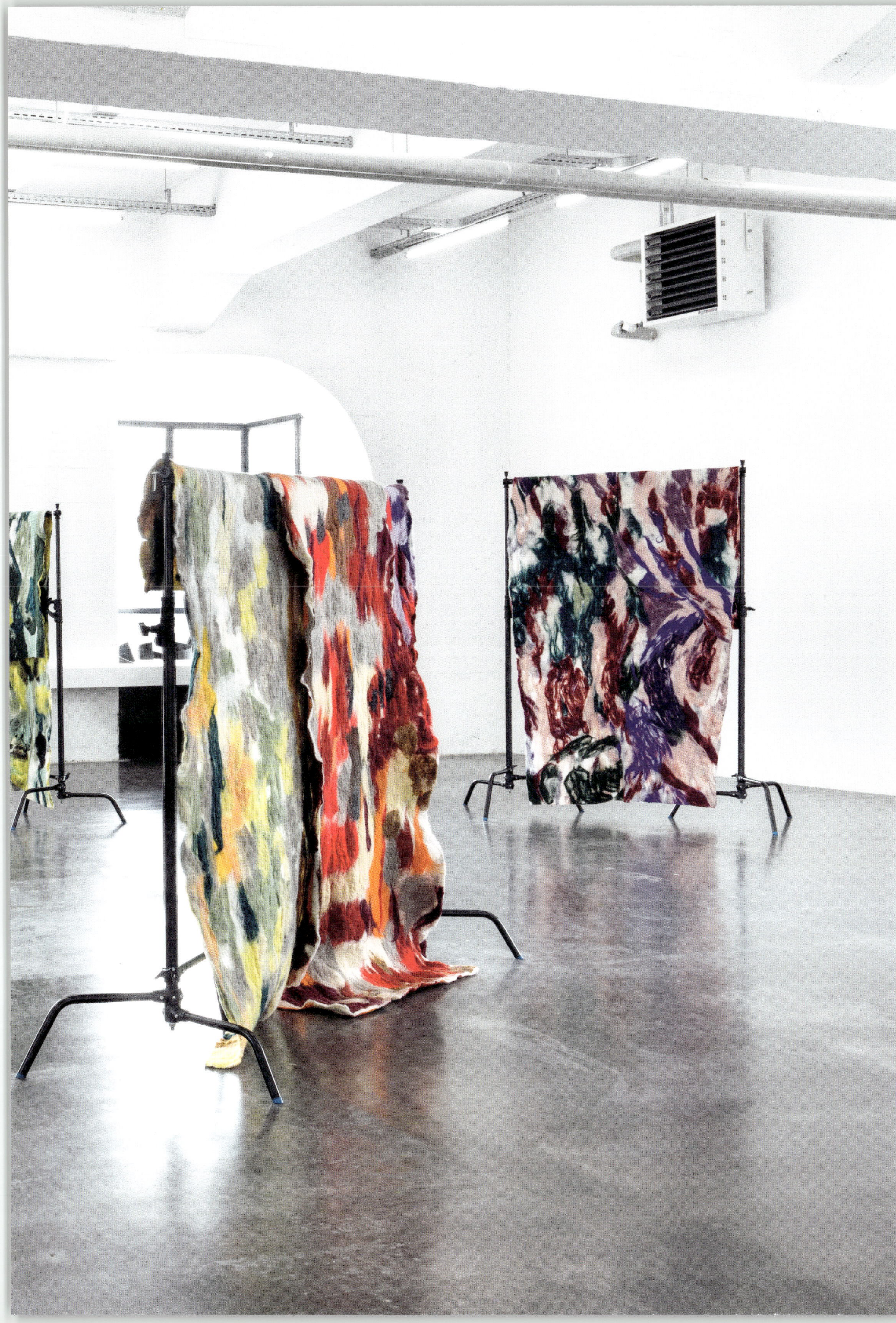

40

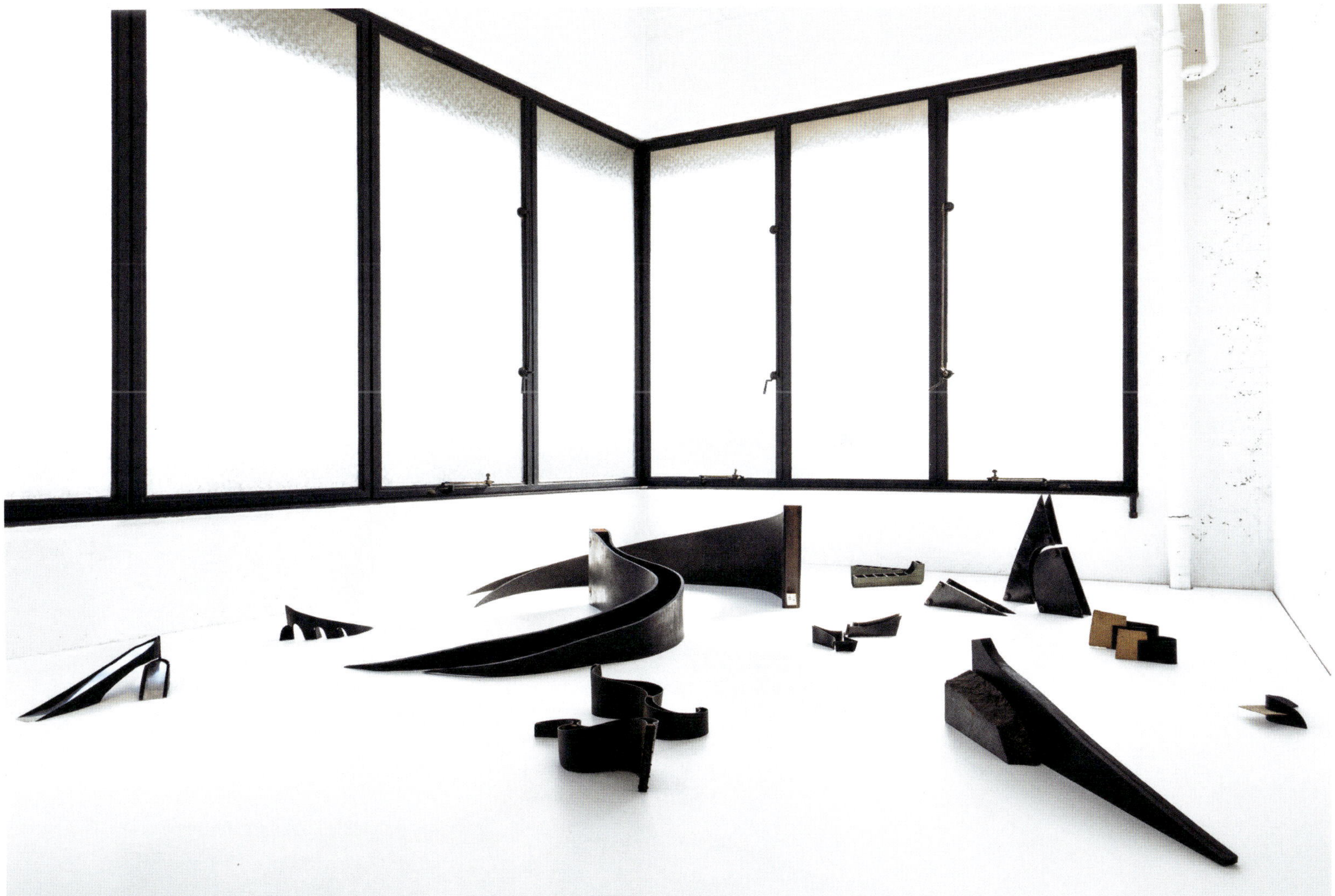

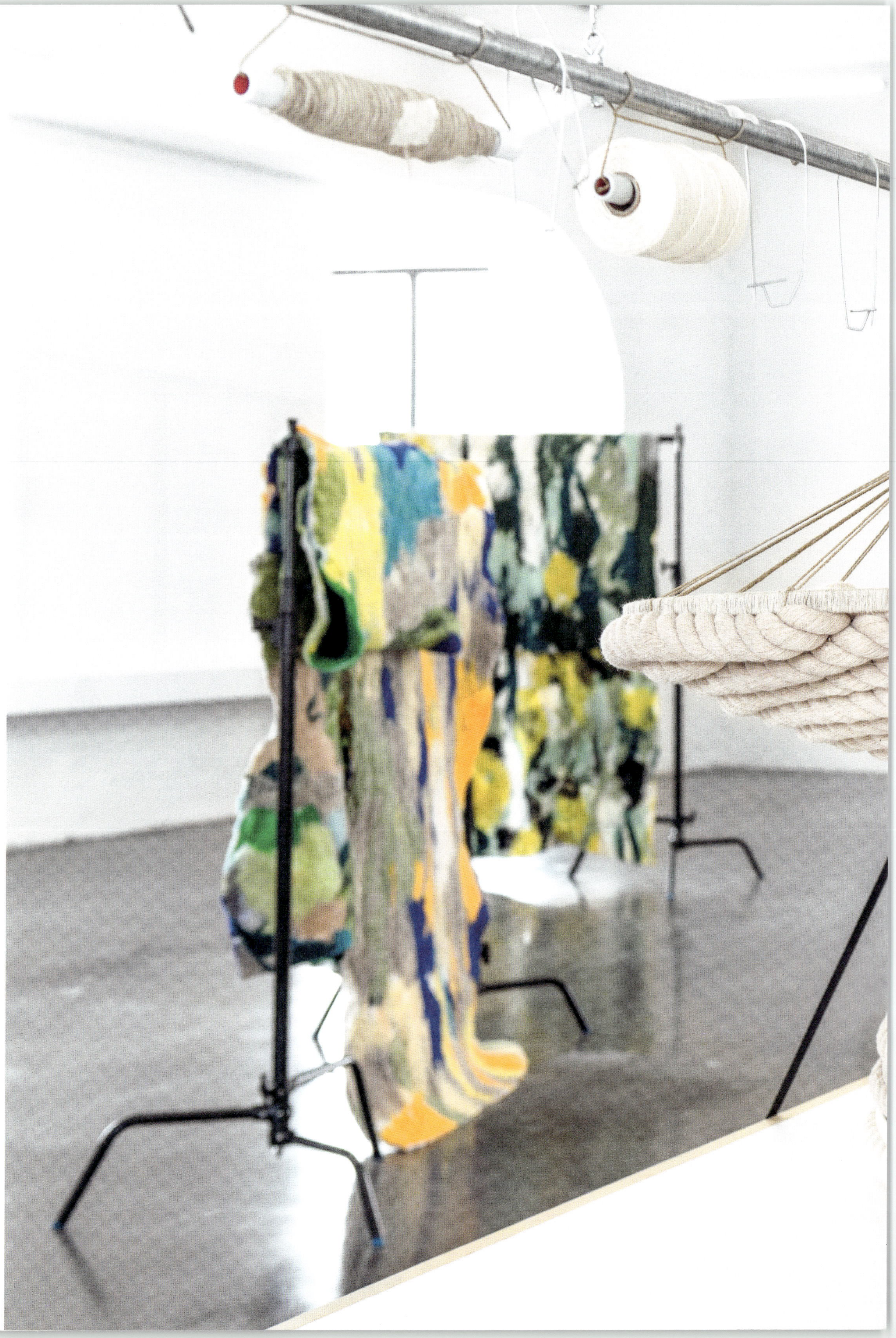

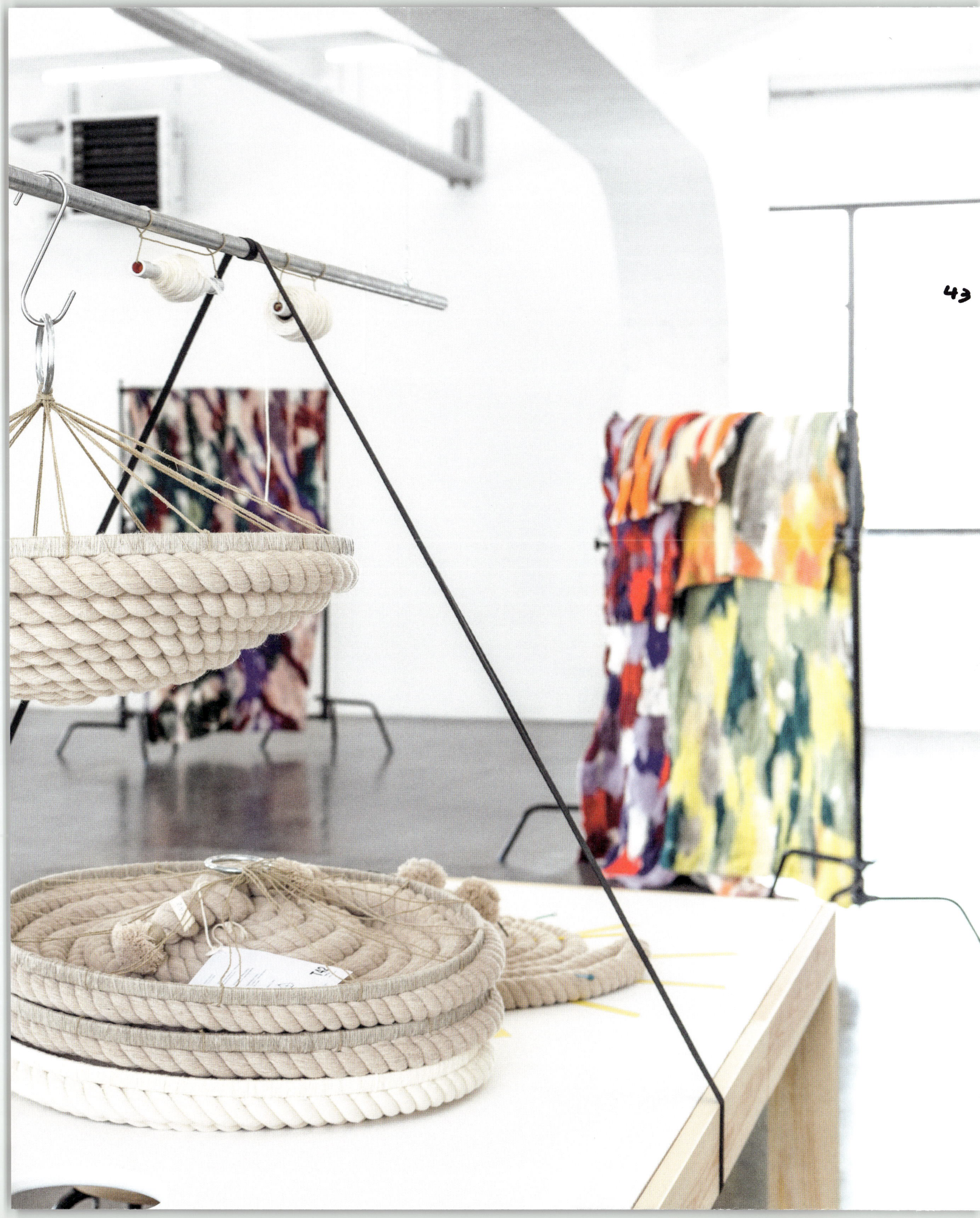

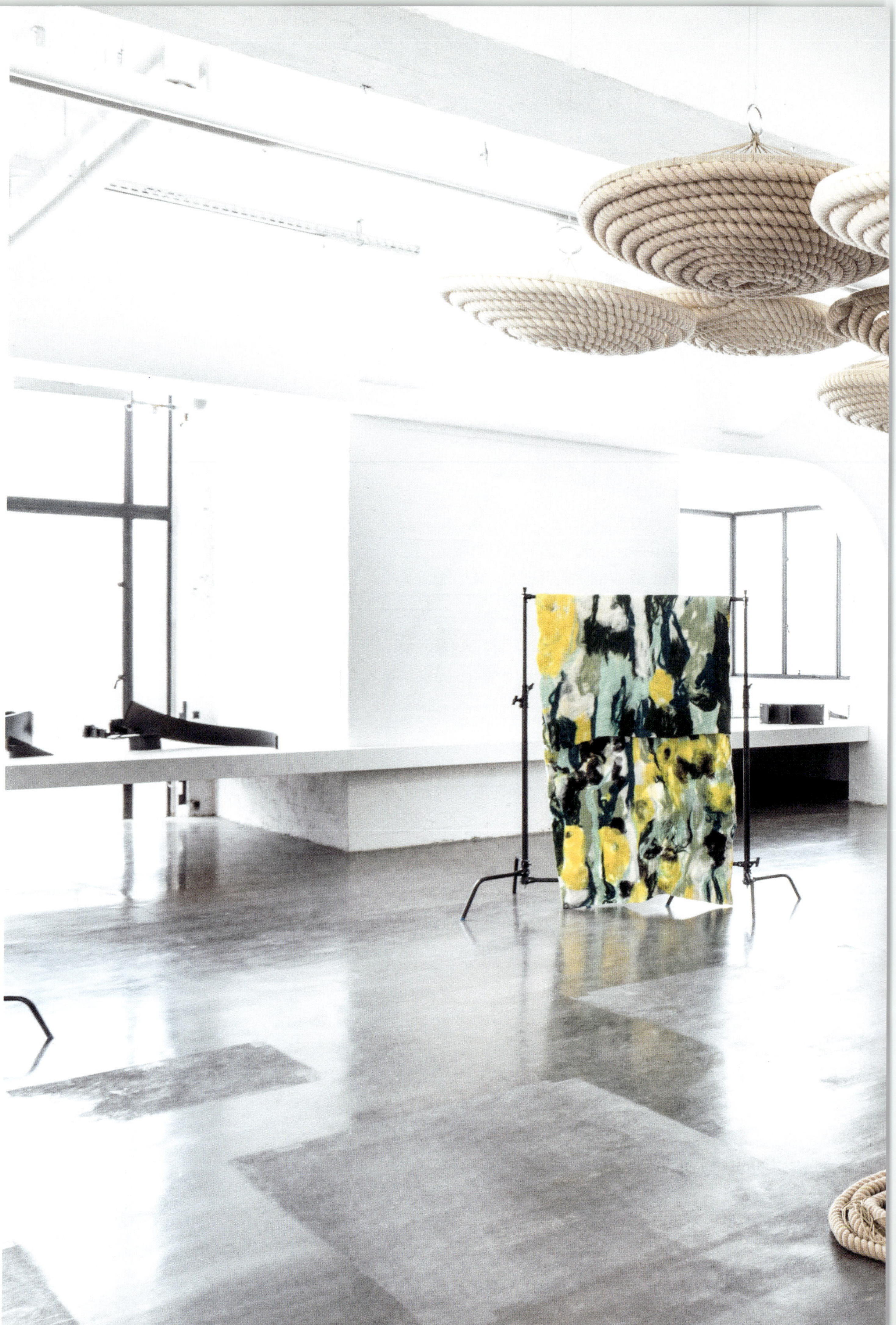

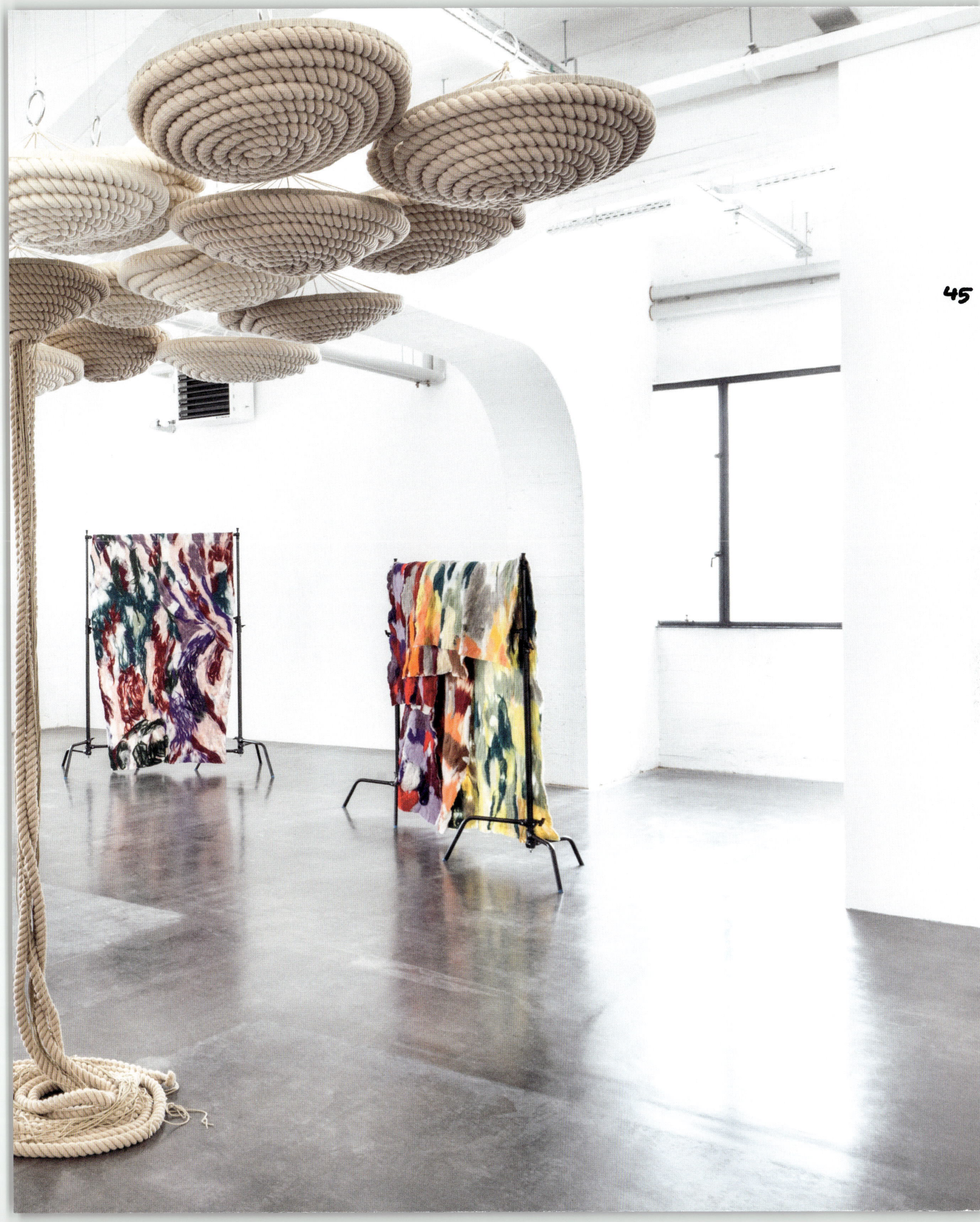

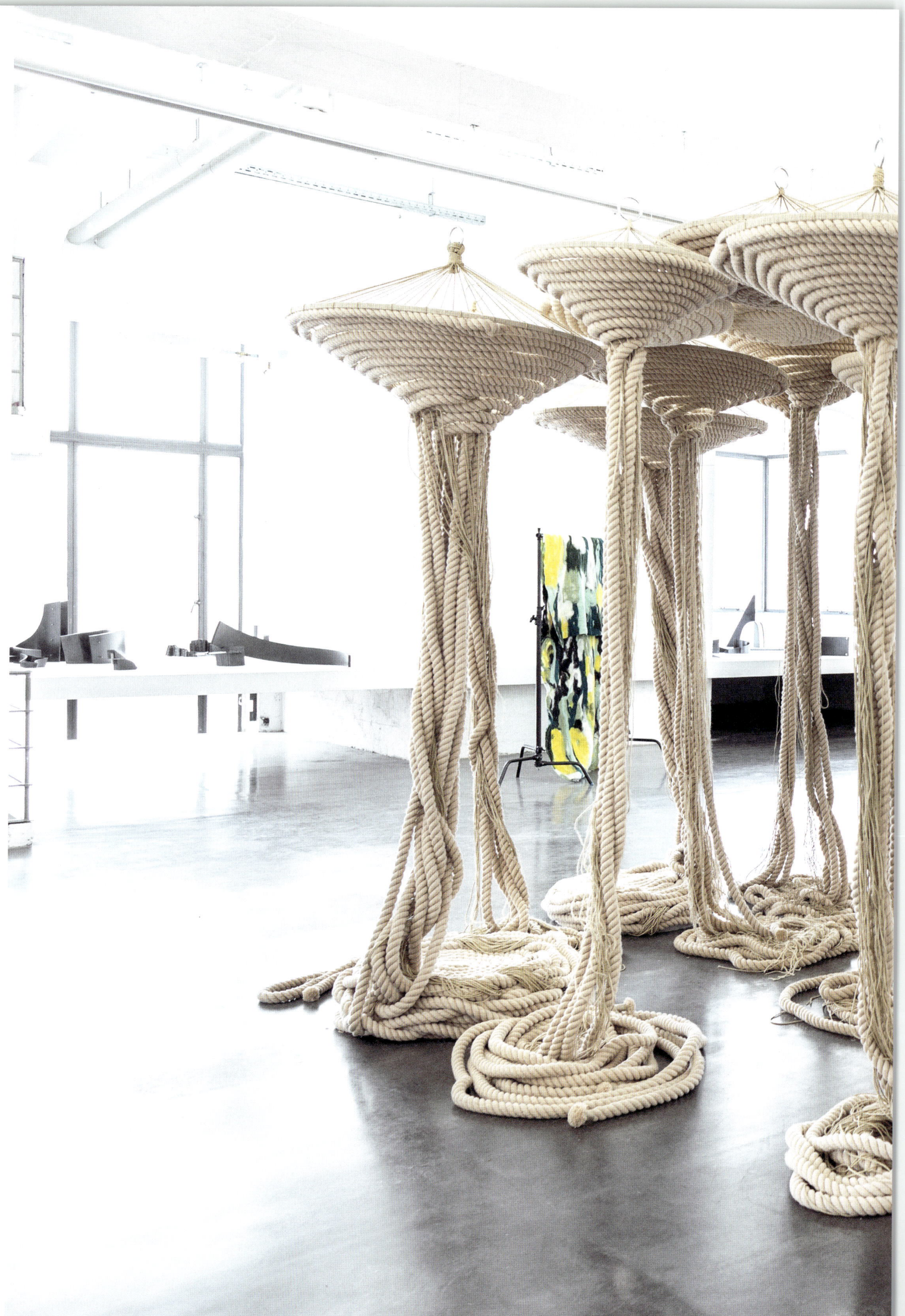

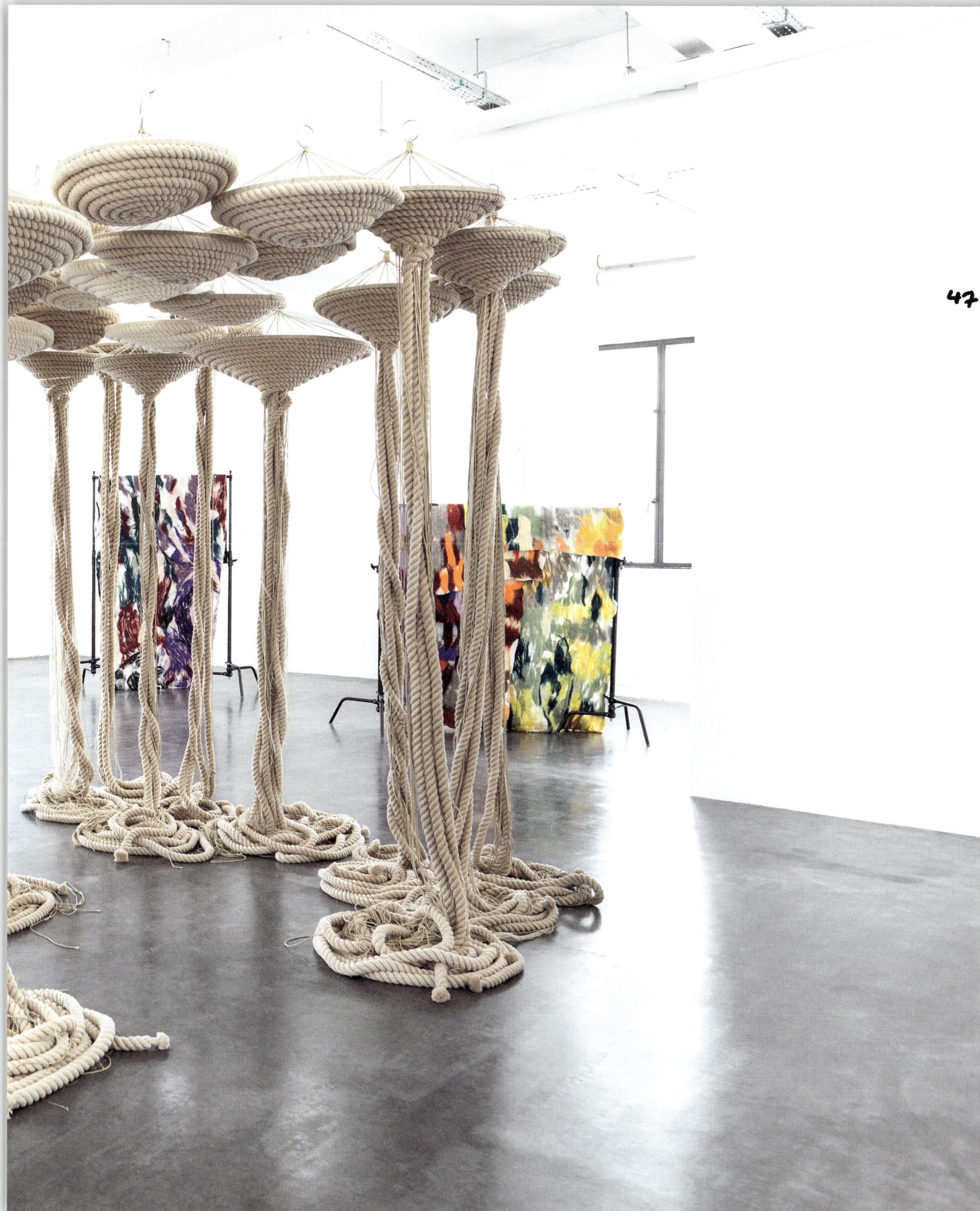

48

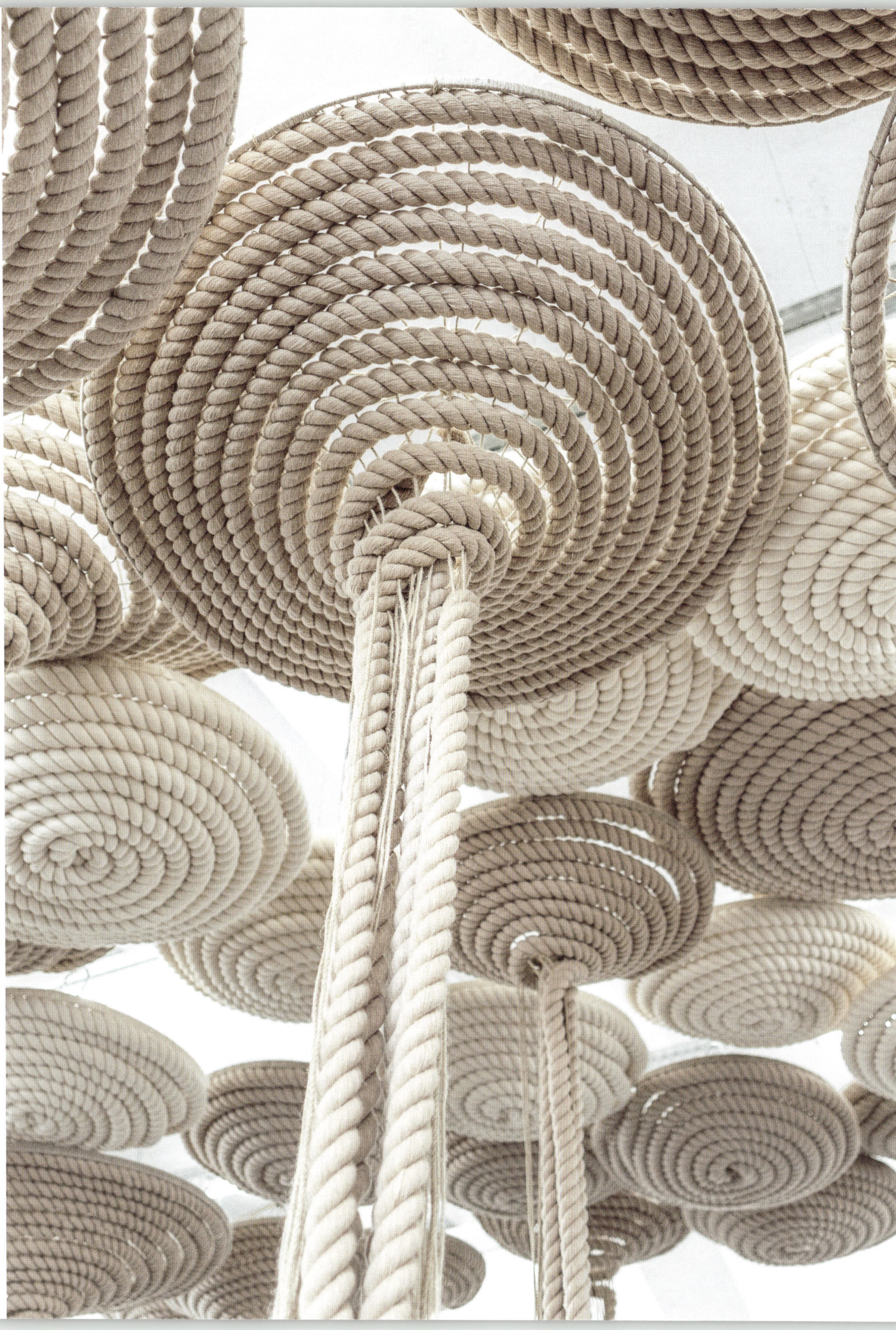

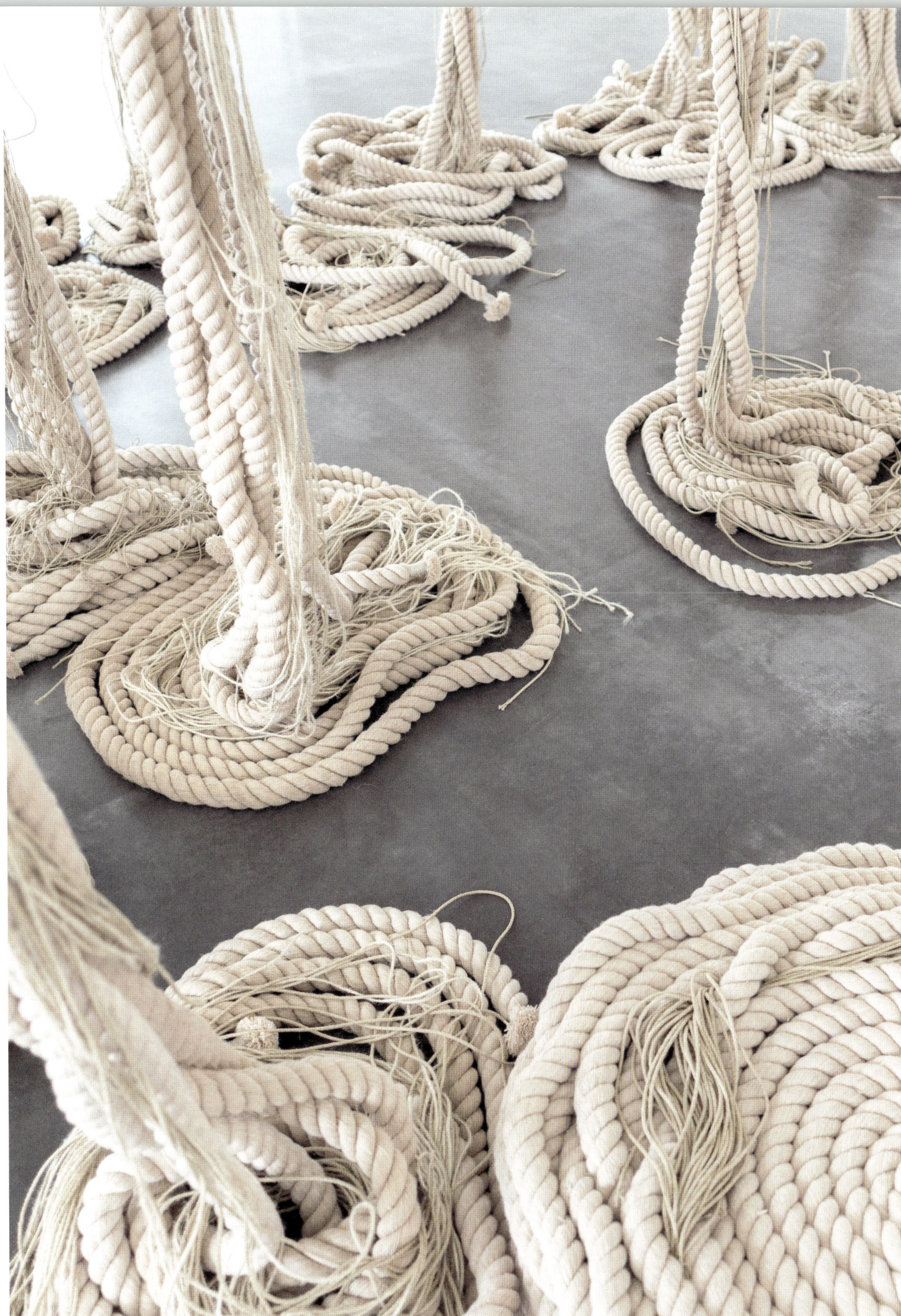

59

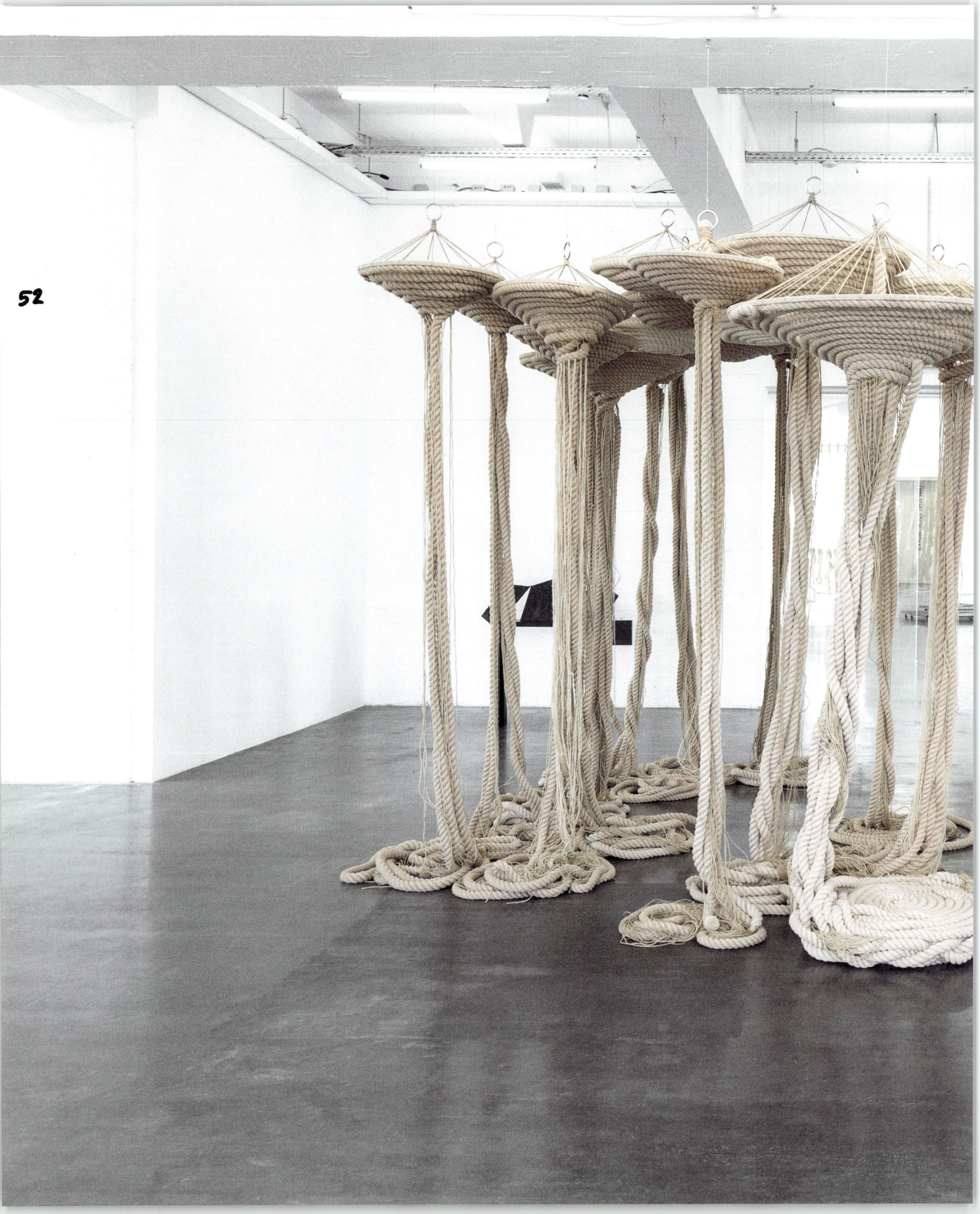

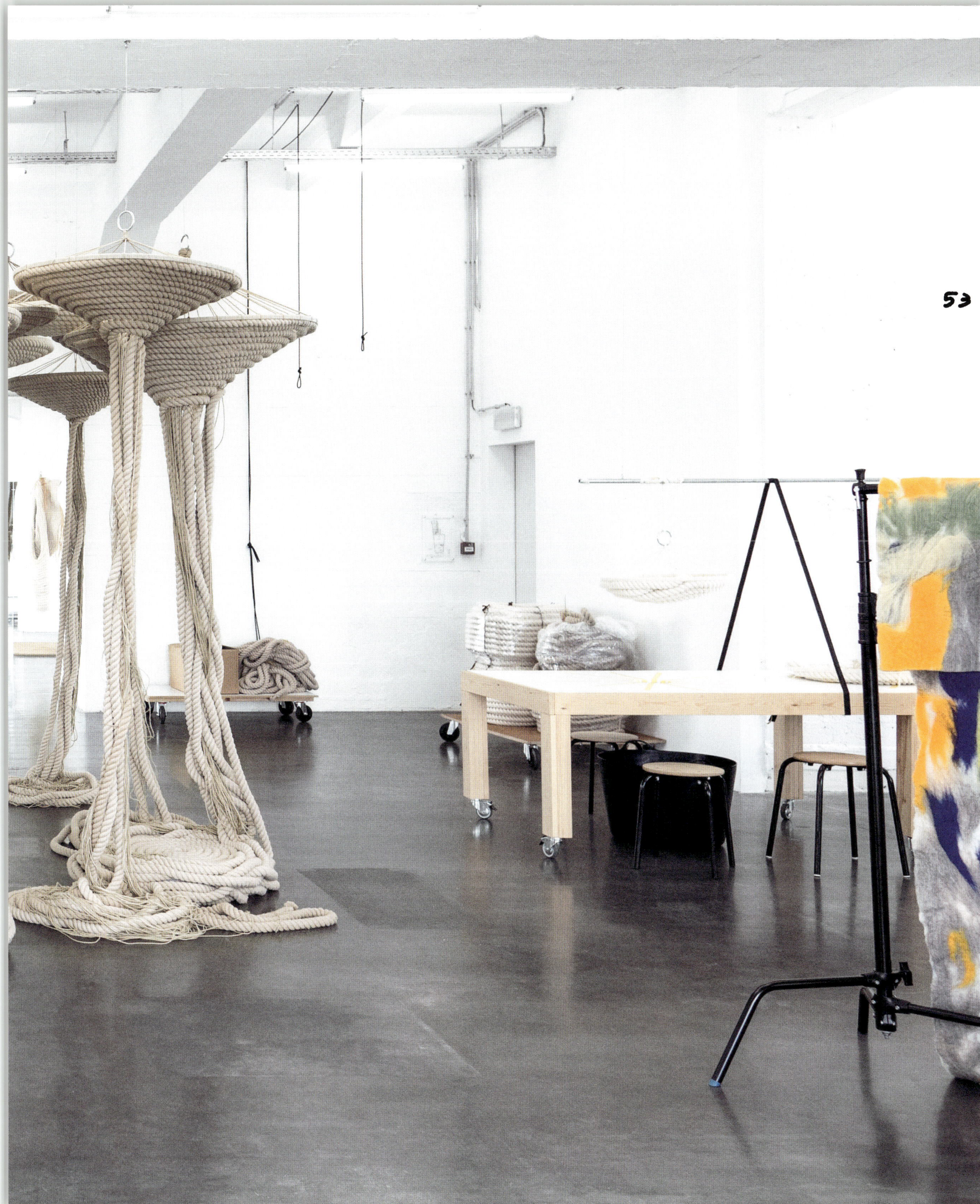

54

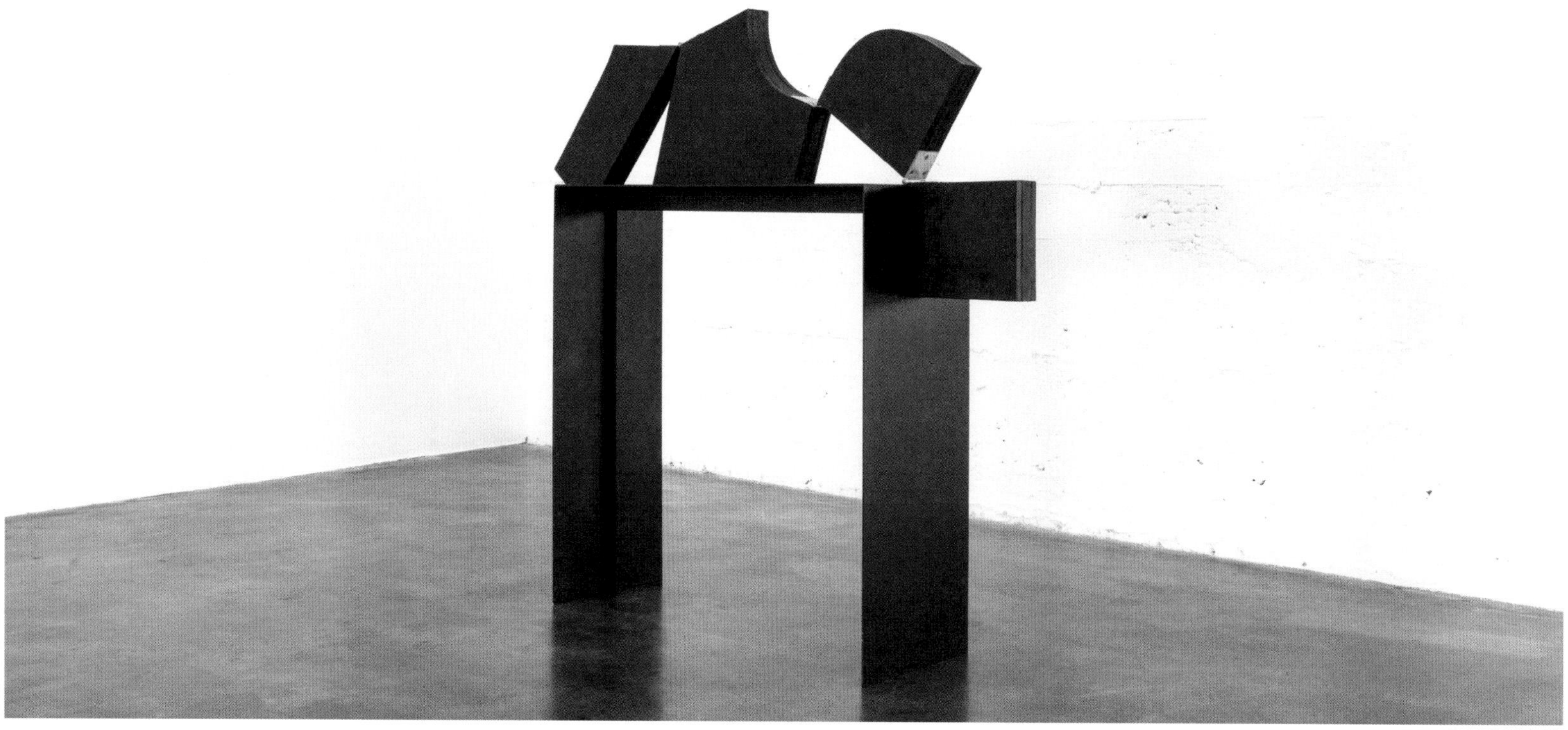

56 preface – Sophie Rocca, Dirk Snauwaert

Our plans for an exhibition about Tapta, which were fueled by conversations with Ann Veronica Janssens, coincided with the research project by Liesbeth Decan, Greet Billet, Hana Miletić and Richard Venlet from LUCA School of Arts on Tapta's artistic influence and legacy. As a result, we didn't hesitate for a moment to give this project a prominent public stage at WIELS, the center for Contemporary Art in Brussels. The proposed project then took on a more concrete form, and evolved from a research project into a dossier-focus exhibition on Tapta, in dialogue with new works by Greet Billet, Hana Miletić and Richard Venlet, each of which addresses some specific aspects of Tapta's practice: her collective, educational practice in the studios in La Cambre and Tournai; the spatialization of forms and patterns; and the manual making process guided by an organic, imperfect and changeable materiality.

It is important to point out Tapta's versatility as a crucial figure in the Belgian/Brussels art scene, as a teacher, and as an idiosyncratic artist. In line with the formalist modernism that her generation professed, she refused to use any anecdotal connection between work and biographical circumstances as an explanation, or to allow herself to be relegated by the postwar political rhetoric to a mere tool. At a time that preceded the debates that drive the generations of today, such as those seeking to bring about a feminist approach towards production and reproduction and to establish the connection between bodily, organic and material elements, Tapta's work and practice was already presenting these elements to us in their early forms and translations. Rather than continuing to base her work on the rigid, closed laws advocated by orthodox formalism, she threw open the constructive imperative to the flexible and changeable of Informalism and — diverging from the regularity and repetition of weaving on the one hand and the robustness of classical sculpture on the other — to a freer use of materials and complexity in the form of cross-links, tensions and bends.

From the beginning, WIELS has been committed to charting and re-evaluating female pioneers within the art world; paradigmatic figures whose influence slowly crystallizes out of the coherence and evolution in their work and with the history of ideas of their time. Even today and notwithstanding the authentic appreciation that a figure such as Tapta received during her lifetime, artists in the neo-avant garde movements here in Belgium are included in surveys only rarely. WIELS aims to help correct those historical records, as it did in 2011 in the case of Alina Szapocznikow, whose works having achieved local publicity in Poland, ultimately gained global recognition. Also, the recent museum retrospectives of Magdalena Abakanowicz's work in neighboring countries form notable indications of the impact that Polish female artists exerted within the post-war diaspora, a group in which Tapta herself ought also to figure prominently.

It is already clear to see that this study will form a stepping stone to a wider survey. To that end, the project is already putting forward the necessary arguments by pointing to parameters such as spatialization, co-creation, a collective experiential space and changeability. Not only did this take place by means of very precisely chosen works, but also by setting up a studio situation in the exhibition in which an exhibition replica was made of Tapta's most monumental surviving work, *Forms for a Flexible Space (Formes pour un espace souple)*, the 1974 original of which is unfortunately in irreparable condition. Partly assisted by advice from Ann Veronica Janssens, Tapta's former assistant, the work was reconstructed using the same techniques and with exactly the same materials and procedures, in a collective studio with textile artists and art students. By applying the co-creation methodology, which Tapta introduced in her "*sculpture souple*" studio at La Cambre, the original, immersive installation gradually emerged and was able be observed and experienced by the public again (p. 44-53).

By showing, as a second focus alongside the textile sculptures, a group of maquettes that Tapta used when conceiving and preparing large public sculptures in neoprene and steel, the exhibition also pays attention to the remarkable rupture within Tapta's oeuvre. In fact, in the 1980s, she gradually abandoned textile and soft materials and techniques for harder and more robust sculptures in black neoprene and steel. It is certainly true to say that this shift led to an uneven appreciation of her work. Today, the textile works are again realizing an easier and more direct connection with viewers, who are invited to embark on a dynamic and sensory journey of discovery as they follow the threads, ropes, knots and torsions. But, notwithstanding the use of large, black, impenetrable surfaces, the neoprene and steel sculptures also allow themselves to be perceived as components of a dynamic, sensory experience, in which the confluences of light on the sliding curves and the subtle reflections and reverberations on the matte surfaces become visible.

This undertaking, which simultaneously includes aspects of art history and awareness-raising, was initiated, and made possible first and foremost by Liesbeth Decan, the curator of the exhibition, and by the artists Greet Billet, Hana Miletić and Richard Venlet, who, by means of their insitu installations, have highlighted, and actualized the features of Tapta's practice cited above.

We also wish to express our thanks in equal measure for the support received from Maurice Verbaet, who immediately made available his collection of works by Tapta; LUCA School of Arts; M HKA; Chevalier-Masson studio, who in collaboration with Estelle Chatelin and Antonella Valerio led the reconstruction of Tapta's *Formes pour un espace souple*; the students and volunteers of ENSAV La Cambre and LUCA School of Arts, who helped produce the reconstruction: Amaryllis Bouyer, Annelies Clerix, Bianca Cuevas Geiger, Rose Egidi, Coline Ernould, Sule Nur Eryuruk, Anouk Ostyn, Marie Rasper, Martha Verleyen; and Gaia Carabillo assisted by Eline Harmse, Korneel Hamers and Yvan Rochette for the construction of the exhibition. We would also like to thank the funding authorities supporting WIELS, the partners and patrons, the members of the WIELS Club and WE Club, as well as the entire WIELS team who shaped this delicate undertaking into a beautiful presentation.

60 Espaces souples – Liesbeth Decan

> "My older sister told me that once, as a little girl, I arranged all my toys in a beautiful circle and started to dance between them and sing: 'I'm Tapta, Tapta, Tapta.' The family liked it, and I became Tapta. Forever." (Tapta, 1997)[1]

Tapta (the pseudonym of Maria Wierusz-Kowalska, born Maria Irena Boyé) was born in Poland in 1926 and came to Belgium as a political refugee with her husband, Krzysztof, after taking part in the Warsaw Uprising of 1944. She studied weaving at the La Cambre National School of Visual Arts, Brussels, from where she graduated in 1949. Shortly afterwards, the couple moved to the Belgian Congo (now Democratic Republic of the Congo), where they lived from 1950 to 1960. On their return to Belgium in 1960, until her sudden death in 1997, she worked in Brussels as an artist and — from 1976 until 1990 — as a professor at La Cambre.

Oddly enough, the above quote about how Tapta got her nickname, and later artist's name, already hints at some of the basic principles within her artistic practice: just as she, as a child, formed a "beautiful circle" with her toys and then began to dance and sing between them, later as an artist she would search for aesthetical shapes that — beyond the purely visual perception — also invite you to move around, between or even into them. It is also the case that however heavy and imposing some of her works may appear, the playful element will always be present.

The ensuing concept of "*sculpture souple*" (flexible sculpture), as Tapta called it, through which an "*espace souple*" (flexible, or supple, space) is created, played a key role in the setup of the exhibition *Tapta: Espaces souples. With Greet Billet, Hana Miletić & Richard Venlet,* of which the current publication is a direct representation. The ideas of spatiality and suppleness (and their interconnection) relate both to the historical oeuvre of Tapta (1926-1997) and the individual contemporary practices of Greet Billet (°1973), Hana Miletić (°1982) and Richard Venlet (°1964), which have been brought together in the exhibition. Furthermore, the two terms should be understood both physically and mentally: the artists' works constitute, or interact with, physical as well as mental spaces, and both a fluidity of matter and a flexibility in thinking and feeling are at play.

From the 1960s onwards, Tapta established herself as an important member of a new generation of artists, who sought to redefine sculpture by using textiles and other flexible materials as sculptural elements. In doing so, she simultaneously took textile art beyond the categories of the decorative arts and crafts. She had her first solo exhibition in 1966 at the Galerie Les Métiers in Brussels, after which her work was shown in major exhibitions in Belgium and abroad, including at the 4th International Biennale of Tapestry in 1969 in Lausanne. This exhibition, in which her work was displayed alongside those of Magdalena Abakanowicz, Jagoda Buić, Elsi Giauque and Sheila Hicks, encouraged her to continue along the path of unconventional experimentation with textiles.

Flexible sculptures

The exhibition *Tapta: Espaces Souples* focused on Tapta's signature works from the 1970s, in which she steadily distanced herself from traditional weaving by applying experimental techniques such as twisting her woven pieces and, in particular, through the use of ropes, which she knotted and joined together into organic volumes. Her work protruded outwards from the wall, became more three-dimensional and increasingly interacted with the space and the viewer, who was invited to experience the works not only visually but also in a tactile and physical manner, stepping around and even inside them.

> "What's my dream? To create softly formed places that envelop you and protect you from the outside world. They become zones of peace and friendship.
>
> What's my dream? To feel enveloped not only by these textile forms, but also by their extensions: large shadows on the walls. That's when real and imaginary, past and future merge and you feel reconciled with everything." (Tapta, 1974)[2]

An early manifestation of these experiments is *Falling Knots (Chute de noeuds*, 1970) (p. 7), consisting of thirteen off-white ropes that are irregularly and intricately knotted and are hanging down over a metal rod. These are no coarse ship's ropes, but soft woolen, cotton and linen ropes that show subtle material differences and invite visitors to touch them. They form a transparent curtain which, when hung against the wall, still refers to classical textile art (or painting, or *bas-relief*), but when hanging in the middle of the room, takes on the allure of a free-standing sculpture — or an anti-sculpture, as it is soft, hanging, transparent, and lying somewhere between a functional curtain and an autonomous work of art.

In 1973, Tapta realized two *Cocoons* (*Cocons*) (p. 8–9, 11, 17, 30), which were displayed together probably for the first time in the exhibition at WIELS. Both pieces are made of undyed cotton ropes sewn together into an organic form, adorned with some sisal strings, loosely hanging down. Underneath is a circular carpet made from ropes of a rougher material (linen or hemp), lying on the floor. The carpets are rugs that are no different from the objects designed for domestic use, but simultaneously function as pedestals that give the sculptures a platform. The sculptures — especially *Cocoon n°1* (p. 8–9) — represent a giant cocoon, a nest. Not just an artwork to contemplate from a distance, but a place in which to shelter, to retreat. (A child said it wanted to crawl into it and read a book there.)

Viewed from another angle (p. 11), the *Cocoons* also represent a larger-than-life vulva — soft and monstruous at the same time — positioning the works within the feminist discourse of the early 1970s. However, this sexualized imagery, reminiscent of the contemporary feminist art movement, is exceptional in Tapta's oeuvre, which is mainly formal and abstract. Tapta's feminism is rather situated in the pursuit of equal appreciation of people of all genders in the art world — "I am an artist, not a woman artist," she often repeated. At the same time, her textile sculptures, including or referencing domestic elements like rugs (in the *Cocoons*), curtains (as in *Falling Knots*), or room dividers (as in *Flexible Horizon*, 1977) (p. 13), another work that was displayed at WIELS), do refer to certain 1970s feminist concerns, such as the elevation of the domestic arts, the dismantling of gendered hierarchies of arts and crafts, and the dignifying of historically feminized labor.[3] Tapta never theorized or pronounced this explicitly, but decisively, almost naturally included high and low in her practice. To her, there existed no hierarchy between creating a monumental sculpture for an exhibition, weaving a poncho for herself or a friend (p. 5, 10), or covering a Bertoia Diamond chair with ropes for her own interior or commissioned by, for example, the Brussels architect Simone Guillissen-Hoa (p. 21). As stated in the quote above, “to create softly formed places that envelop you and protect you from the outside world, [that] become zones of peace and friendship” is what she wanted to achieve.

If the *Cocoons* are not designed to be physically entered, then at least the round carpet will stimulate you to walk around it. This way, visual perception is accompanied by a physical experience; you cannot fully see the work without moving around it, as each side of it is different and equally interesting. Tapta invites a physical, tactile approach to her works, and this is also how they come about: not through sketches on paper, but by means of scale models, executed in the material of the ultimate artwork. Manipulating the material leads her to the final form of the work.

Weaving through the space

Tapta’s activation of the viewer also manifests itself in the black neoprene works that she began to make in the late 1980s and which — following an intermediate phase of experimenting with rubber and stretching ropes across the vaults of the exhibition spaces — marked a radical and final turn in her use of materials. Handcrafted rope sculptures now gave way to sculptures and installations from the industrially manufactured material, neoprene. Large black surfaces connected by metal bars and bolts form open structures, through or past which the viewer has to walk. Sometimes, the different elements of the sculpture are connected by hinges, allowing their shape to be changed — according to the size of the space or the will of the visitor.

This applies to two works in the exhibition: *Impatient* (*Impatiente,* 1995) (p. 4–5), a large floor sculpture on small wheels that could be transformed from a square of 2 x 2 meters into a chain of larger and smaller geometrical planes, and an untitled work (1994) (p. 54), which is placed on a metal base, and consists of four neoprene elements which — connected by hinges — can take different forms. Moreover, according to Tapta, it is precisely by manipulating and by changing the sculpture's shape using our own hands that we start to understand it: "I'm now working on playful pieces: mobile, articulated, hinged, that can move, that you can touch. (…) These are all geometric shapes cut into smaller pieces, that can be assembled and disassembled, that you can also understand by manipulating."[4]

Learning by touching. This method is also reflected in her preparation process. As in the case of the textile sculptures, Tapta invented her neoprene sculptures by making scale models in the same material. The exhibition featured several dozen small models in neoprene, positioned on knee-high platforms in the three niches in the back of the exhibition space (p. 33, 35, 41). The models are miniature versions of the final monumental works, or trial versions of sculptures that were never executed. They show cuttings and curves that foreshadow how, in the eventual installations, Tapta would lead, or weave, the visitors through the space, making them experience the environment differently. She envisioned the "metamorphosis of a space by introducing a supple, flexible element"; "developing a new dynamism in the space."[5]

Responding to this key element of her oeuvre, Richard Venlet created *Salon II* (p. 1, 2–3, 18–19, 20–21, 30–31), a transparent, flexible wall structure with three doorways that guided the visitors past Tapta's works and through the space. Simultaneously fulfilling the role of a scenographic intervention and of an autonomous artwork, *Salon II* generated a fluid spatial, visual, and tactile experience. As the artist himself puts it further in this volume (p. 75), the structure nestled itself "chameleonically" in the exhibition space, between the works. That way, it intensified the activation of the viewer, of the works displayed, and of the spatial environment, that was pioneered by Tapta. More specifically, Venlet's structure continues the idea of "passage," which Tapta developed in installations such as *Place of Transition* (*Lieu de Transition*, 1987, for M HKA) or *Transit* (1991, Open Air Museum Sart-Tilman, Liège) (p. 75). In terms of materiality though, his work, made of thin, transparent plexi sheets kept together by transparent zip ties, is the exact opposite to the opaque black neo-

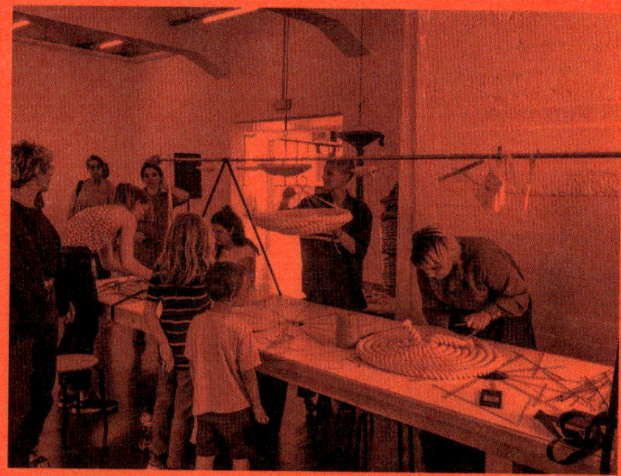 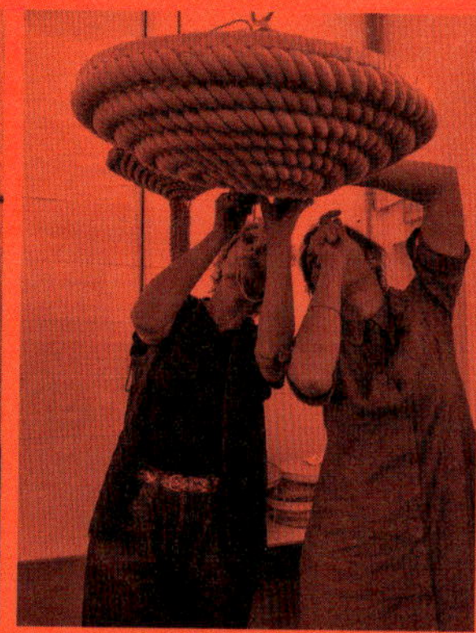 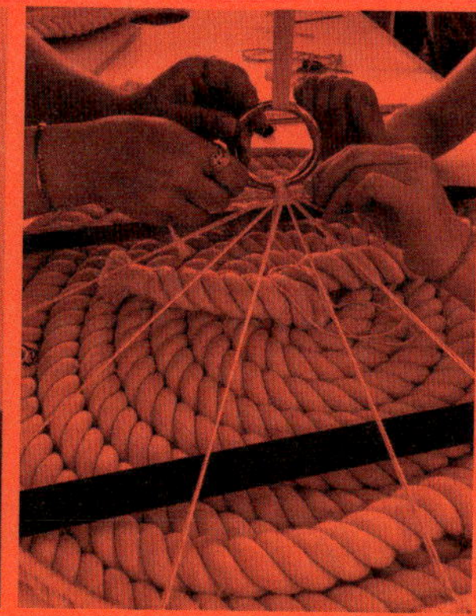

prene surfaces that Tapta used in those installations, and rather hints at Tapta's interest, in the latter part of her career, in the use of mirrors, water, and light projections.

> "Now I'm starting to work a little with light, which is the opposite of opacity. Opacity is the search for the strongest contrast in the environment. When they're opaque, the black contours, both on the outside and on the inside, have more presence (...) now I want to punch a hole in that, even if the black is already a black hole." (Tapta, 1993)[6]

Greet Billet's work also refers to these late works incorporating light and water. Among other parallels that she discovered between her own and Tapta's practice (as explained by her later on in this catalog) (p. 71–72), both artists often work(ed) in situ, creating installations in which artwork and environment interact. Here, two large mirror works were hung on either side of the exhibition entrance. The work, entitled *Réfléchir (à) Tapta* (2023) (p. 6, 22–23), refers on the one hand to the figure of the triangle, which Tapta included in several neoprene installations in the 1990s, and on the other hand to Tapta's use of mirrors and especially mirrored water surfaces as in the temporary installation at Galerie Tilman in Brussels in 1996, or the public sculpture *Open Mind* (*Esprit Ouvert,* 1997) near the Brussels North Station. Like Tapta's installations incorporating still water surfaces, Billet's triangles reflect the exhibition, thereby merging as an artwork, with the works by the other artists, as well as with the visitors and the surrounding space, and also capturing its changing dynamics, including the movements of the visitors, and the altering light conditions.

Co-creation

Perhaps the most innovative part of Tapta's oeuvre are her environments from the early 1970s. Made of ropes strung together into "flexible spaces" (*espaces souples*), they are a kind of soft, fluid rooms or tents, in which the viewer can enter and take a seat. These structures, both open and secure, serve as resting and meeting places where, alone or together with acquaintances or strangers, one can pause, be quiet or engage in conversation.

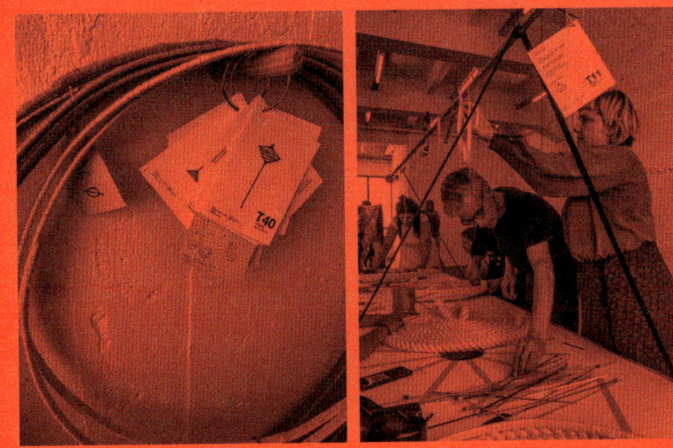

Reconstruction studio of Tapta's *Formes pour un espace souple* in the exhibition *Tapta: Espaces souples*, WIELS, Brussels, 18 May - 13 August 2023, led by Chevalier-Masson studio, in collaboration with Estelle Chatelin and Antonella Valerio, and students and volunteers from ENSAV La Cambre and LUCA School of Arts.

As far as we know, only one of these impressive installations still survives: *Forms for a Flexible Space* (*Formes pour un espace souple,* 1974), which Tapta donated to the Gordon Matta Clark Foundation in 1975 and is now in the M HKA collection. Due to careless preservation in the past, however, the work is in extremely poor condition. After consultation with textile conservators who examined the work, and artist Ann Veronica Janssens, former student and assistant of Tapta, and in order to be able to publicly display the work again in the future, we decided to make a reconstruction of the installation in the exhibition in WIELS. Led by the Chevalier-Masson studio, in collaboration with Estelle Chatelin and Antonella Valerio, students and volunteers from ENSAV La Cambre and LUCA School of Arts realized the exhibition copy, using the same materials and following the same techniques as Tapta and her assistants had applied.[7]

As a result of the curatorial decision to position the reconstruction studio in the exhibitions space, the process-related and collective experience that Tapta pursued was made tangible again. Moreover, Tapta's idea of *Sculpture Souple* was extended to the exhibition, which — as the production of the work progressed — also changed in form. Indeed, as the installation grew larger (p. 44-45, 46-47), Hana Miletić's works were arranged differently, in dialogue with Tapta's works and the space.

The reconstruction studio also refers to Tapta's teaching. All interviews with the artist and testimonials from people who knew her attest to the fact that she considered her teaching activities to be as important as her artistic practice. In 1976, Tapta was appointed as a professor at the La Cambre National School of Advanced Visual Arts, where, until 1990, she headed the "Textile Design" workshop, renaming it "Flexible Sculpture" *(Sculpture Souple)*. Rather than instructing her students in a particular technique, she prioritized the development of an open and critical mind. Her students included Ann Veronica Janssens, Monica Droste and Marie-Jo Lafontaine. From approx. 1979 to approx. 1987, Janssens and Droste were also her assistants and helped to create Tapta's textile sculptures based on her scale models. From 1980 onwards and besides teaching at La Cambre, Tapta also coordinated the "Structure" studio of the Fondation de la Tapisserie in Tournai, which later became

TAMAT (Musée de la Tapisserie et des Arts Textiles de la Fédération Wallonie-Bruxelles). All these engagements bear witness to her deep commitment to mentoring and encouraging young artists in particular.

An interesting aspect of her pedagogics was that she motivated students to participate in co-creation projects, alongside their individual practices. Here too, as in Tapta's own oeuvre, the emphasis lies upon the interaction between the hands and the materials, between the different creators, and between the artwork and its "users" (for example, the children who played in the structures). Inspired by these tactile and playful installations, and in collaboration with Espace Fxmme-Globe Aroma and the public, Hana Miletić created new works within their series of *Felt workshops* (2018) (p. 36–37, 38–39). These multicolored textiles, presented hanging on black metal stands, were made during collaborative workshops, in which participants are guided through the technique of wet felting, a manual technique, a fact that Miletić emphasizes (p. 73) and which revalues gendered cultural practices. Three felts were made on site at WIELS — one together with its staff, and two others with the participants of two public workshops — and were added to the installation during the course of the exhibition. By facilitating new connections between working, thinking and feeling, Miletić's work connects with the methodology of Tapta, whose "supple sculptures" came about first of all through the manipulation of and careful "listening to" her materials, and subsequently as a result of their multisensory interaction with the public and the exhibition space.

I hope that by creating this exhibition, we have succeeded in showing the connecting power of Tapta's multifaceted practice, which not only consisted of creating autonomous artworks, applied objects such as garments and furniture, and works situated somewhere in between the two, but also of teaching and initiating collaborative projects. By making this exhibition and having been particularly inspired by Julia Bryan-Wilson's book *Fray: Art + Textile Politics* (2017), I understood that all these registers of making play a "crucially coconstitutive" role within Tapta's practice and form its layered meaning.[8]

1 Tapta, in an interview with Wiesława Wierzchowska, published in *Pokaz*, no.21, 1997, p. 13. Original quote: "Kiedyś, jako malutka dziewczynka (opowiadała mi to starsza siostra), ustawiłam wszystkie swoje zabawki w piękny krąg, zaczęłam między nimi tańczyć i śpiewać: 'jestem Tapta, Tapta, Tapta.' Rodzinie się to spodobało i zostałam Tapta. Na zawsze." An English translation of the interview was published first in Greet Billet, Liesbeth Decan & Hana Miletic (eds), *Tapta*, Warsaw: Arton Foundation, 2021: 93-99.

2 Tapta in *Triënnale 3*, exhib. cat., Bruges, Beurshalle, 1974, n.p. Original quote: "Mon rêve? Créer des lieux aux formes molles, qui vous enveloppent et vous protègent du monde extérieur. Elles deviennent des zones de calme et d'amitié. Mon rêve? Se sentir envelope non seulement par ses formes textiles, mais également par leurs prolongements: de grandes ombres sur les murs. Alors le reel et l'imaginaire, le passé et le future, ce (sic) confondent, et on se sent réconcilié avec le tout."

3 Here, I am transposing Julia Bryan-Wilson's analysis of Harmony Hammond's *Floorpieces* from her book *Fray: Art + Textile Politics* (The University of Chicago Press, 2017, p. 75), to Tapta's use of domestic elements.

4 Michel Baudson, *Tapta. Conversations, mars-décembre 1993*, Brussels, Artgo, 1994, p. 37. Original quote: "(...) je travaille maintenant sur des pièces ludiques: c'est à dire mobiles, articulées, à charnières, qui peuvent bouger, que l'on pourra toucher. (...) Ce sont toutes des formes géométriques découpées en plus petits morceaux, qui s'assemblent et se désassemblent, que l'on pourra comprendre aussi par la manipulation."

5 Preparatory project of *Place of Transition (Lieu de transition)* for the exhibition *Inside-Outside* at MUHKA, Antwerp, 1987 (Archives M HKA). Original quotes: "métamorphose d'un espace par introduction d'un élément souple, flexible", "développer un nouveau dynamisme de l'espace."

6 Baudson, 1994, p. 18. Original quote: "Maintenant, je commence un peu à travailler avec la lumière qui est le contraire de l'opacité. L'opacité, c'est la recherche du contraste le plus fort dans l'environnement. Quand ils sont opaques, les contours noirs, aussi bien à l'extérieur qu'à l'intérieur, ont plus de présence (...) j'ai envie maintenant de trouer cela, même si le noir est déjà un trou noir."

7 The students and volunteers of ENSAV La Cambre and LUCA School of Arts who helped manufacture the exhibition copy of *Forms for a Flexible Space (Formes pour un espace souple)* were Amaryllis Bouyer, Annelies Clerix, Bianca Cuevas Geiger, Rose Egidi, Coline Ernould, Sule Nur Eryuruk, Anouk Ostyn, Marie Rasper and Martha Verleyen.
The reconstruction was not entirely finished at the end of the exhibition (as the last photos of the work show) but was finished afterwards and will be premiered at Muzeum Susch, Switzerland, during the summer of 2024.

8 Bryan-Wilson, 2017, p. 41.

9 Raymond Balau, "Entretien avec Tapta, A propos de l'installation à la Galerie Etienne Tilman", *Flux-news*, Liège, Belgium, no.10, August 1996, p.5. Original quote: "Le jour, la rue entrait dans mon espace. La nuit au contraire, elle paraissait très éloignée."

70 Greet Billet, Hana Miletić and Richard Venlet on tapta

Greet Billet

What did you make for the exhibition?

I wanted to create a work that would relate not only to Tapta's oeuvre, but also to the visitors and the exhibition space itself. That was the reason why I decided to produce an insitu installation, which is where the focus of my artistic practice lies. After researching Tapta's oeuvre and having made multiple visits to the space, I finally arrived at a design for two large triangular mirrors. Each of these takes the form of two identical right-angled triangles measuring 4300 x 2300 x 4876 x 6 mm. The dimensions were partly determined by the area of the wall and of the exhibition space itself.

What was your starting point, to which part of Tapta's practice does your work respond?

The starting point for *Réfléchir (à) Tapta* (2023) are the sculptures that Tapta realized by means of light projections, such as *Cutting Through the Intangible* (*Tailler dans l'impalpable*, 1993). However, I was particularly and primarily intrigued by the insitu installation that Tapta created at Etienne Tilman's gallery in Brussels in 1996. This consisted of two sculptures in neoprene, resembling flying buttresses standing on the ground and leaning against the wall, combined with a wooden square painted black and a white triangle projected on the wall. Tapta went one step further by flooding the gallery space with water, creating a huge reflective surface that de-duplicated the work.

I discovered this work when I came across a small black-and-white photograph in the archives of the Royal Museums of Fine Arts in Brussels and was totally fascinated as soon as I saw it. Several aspects of this work are intangible, which, in my view, gives it an almost mythical character. Indeed, the work itself only endures in the form of photographs and in the memories of those who saw it at the time. The immateriality of the light projection and of the reflection of the material almost cause it to merge with the space for which it was made.

In this work, I can observe a few similarities to my own practice, including the insitu aspect, projection, reflection, monochromy and the contrast between light and dark. Initially, I planned to adopt all these aspects almost verbatim. However, it is very strange how differently you look at the space and how many facets of it you discover when no exhibition is taking place there at the time, or when you know you will be exhibiting there yourself and visit the space several times by way of preparation. One of the things I discovered was that it already contained many of the elements I wanted to include in my design, which therefore eliminated the need to translate them into my own work. The floor of the exhibition hall is dark gray and reflects the light much more than I had ever noticed before. Following discussions with the curator and the other artists, we decided to make all the windows visible, to remove the false walls from previous exhibitions and the light filters in front of the window glass, and to leave the walls in "neutral" white. As a result, we succeeded in obtaining fantastic light. Moreover, WIELS' industrial architecture is no stranger to Tapta's

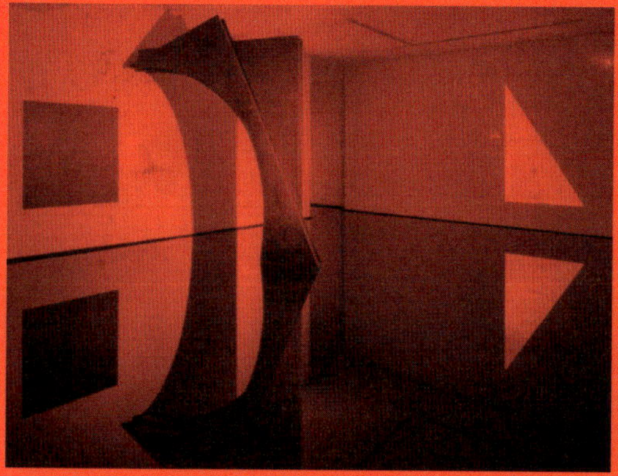 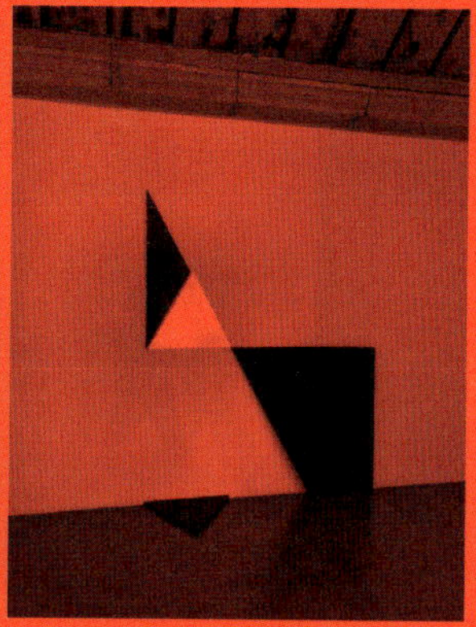

Left: Tapta, Untitled, 1996, Installation view at Galerie Etienne Tilman, Brussels.
Right: Tapta, *Tailler dans l'Impalpable (Cutting through the Intangible)*, 1993, neoprene, metal, light projection, 245 x 170 x 45 cm. (Collection Maurice Verbaet)

72 aesthetic. The space itself already embodied the properties of reflection, monochromy and the contrast between light and dark, so I felt I could omit those from my own design. The right-angled triangle remained, and since the use of mirrors refers not only to Tapta's work but also to my own practice, I thought this was the most appropriate material to execute them in. The two triangles are identical and together form a rectangle, which can also be regarded as a reference to Tapta's practice. The reflection of the space ensuing from the work, Tapta's works and the visitors walking past them played a key role in my quest to achieve the "right" installation.

How would you describe the relationship between your work and that of Tapta?

I can see several connections between Tapta's work and my own; I even discovered chronological similarities in the way they were conceived and developed. While studying Printmaking I tried to take the medium of printmaking out of its small-scale format and create very large three-dimensional works with it. That connection between scaling up and the desire to make a two-dimensional technique three-dimensional is an aspect that I have also encountered in Tapta's works. In her textile works, that scaling-up manifests itself in the fact that she weaves and knots together thick cords instead of the usual thinner weaves. To my mind, this marks the beginning of the process by which she starts turning her two-dimensional weaving into three-dimensional flexible structures. Also, similar to the works she created in neoprene, I feel the need to create large and spatial sculptures using flexible materials. An additional similarity also relates to the use of color, or, more specifically in the ordering of color. In works such as *Flexible Horizon (Horizon flexible,* 1976) (p. 13) and *Untitled* (1982) (p. 16), both of which are included in this exhibition, as well as in other works, you can see that Tapta is organizing color by means of a "dégradé", in other words, from light to dark. I obtained the same arrangement of color by means of translations from digital to analog. Tapta, like me, also values reflection and light, which can be so defining but also so changeable within one space. In an interview following her work at Galerie Etienne Tilman, she said, "By day, the street entered my space. At night, on the contrary, it seemed far away."[7] I completely understand what she meant. In my case, the same works can even be completely different, depending on the space in which they are exhibited. The idea behind the above quotation is also that Tapta needs to adapt her work to the space itself and to its in-built sense of light, and that need is something that I feel too. I can also observe similarities to my own practice in Tapta's use of soft materials. She initially uses wool, silk, cotton, sisal and so on to weave with and with which to create large spatial sculptures and structures, but the neoprene she later uses in her installations is a flexible material as well. I also set out to exploit the inherent characteristics of materials when using plexiglass, which bends due to its weight, or in types of film that are already thin and flexible and therefore embody a movement and shape of their very own. In addition to all this, I feel a kind of kinship with Tapta as

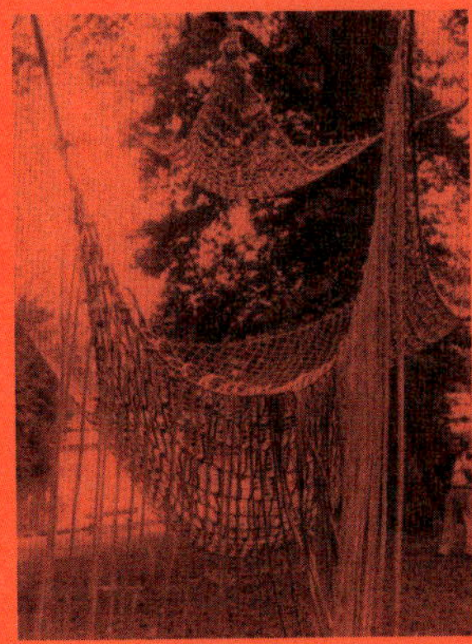

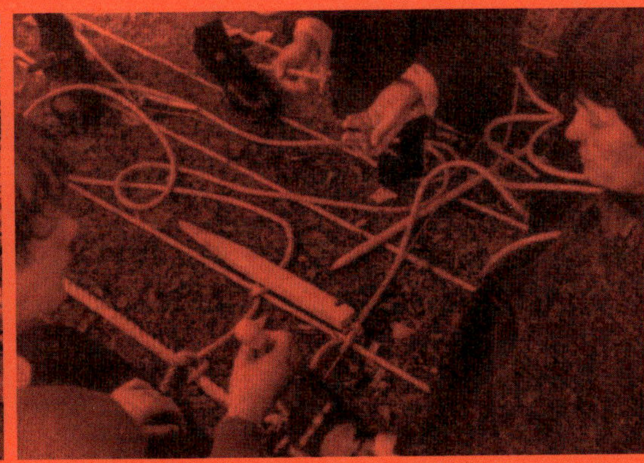

Structure spontanée (Spontaneous Structure), Installation made by Tapta in collaboration with her students from La Cambre for a group of elementary school children, 1978, Manila hemp. Part of the exhibition *Tapisseries d'aujourd'hui*, Woluwe-Saint-Lambert: Château Malou. Photographs from Françoise Galle & Marie-Paule Ripoche, "Tapta" in *Dri a di*, 9, April 1979, p.18.

a person. Indeed, I am in awe of the way in which she functioned as a woman with children in a male-dominated art world and to the methodology that she applied in her teaching.

Hana Miletić

What did you make for the exhibition?

Together with different groups of people, and during the course of an 18-month period, I produced an ensemble of nine multicolored, hand-felted textiles (approximately 150 x 300 x 2 cm/felt) that were draped over five metal backdrop stands and spread out in the second gallery room of the exhibition. These felts were made during a series of *Felt workshops* that took place at the Kunsthalle Mainz (in the winter of 2022-2023), in Globe Aroma, Brussels (in spring 2023) and at WIELS, Brussels (in the summer of 2023). *Felt workshops* are hands-on, collaborative, public workshops during which participants are guided through the technique of wet felting, a manual production technique that revalues gendered cultural practices. Since 2017, I have been collaborating for the facilitation of the *Felt workshops* with Espace Fxmme, a group of women and non-binary people working in the Globe Aroma community arts center in Brussels.

Wool felt is one of the oldest manufactured textiles. It does not require any tools other than one's hands. Hot water and soap are applied to layers of wool, while tender massaging and pressing causes the fibers to become permanently entangled to form a single piece of fabric. The multitude of hands and voices in the *Felt workshops* lend them a micro-political capacity that is poetically reflected in the technique of wet felting. The differently colored parts of the felt are still distinguishable, but up close you can see how they are gently intertwined.

The installation consisting of hand-felted textiles grew during the exhibition: Three felts were made on site at WIELS, together with its team, and with the participants of two public workshops. The raw wool used during these workshops refers to the colors of the exhibited works by Tapta. The installation also moved through the gallery room in relation to the evolving recreation of *Forms fora Flexible Space (Formes pour un Espace Souple)*, Tapta's emblematic fiber environment from 1974.

What was your starting point, or to which part of Tapta's practice does your work respond?

I wanted to respond to Tapta's educational projects that took place outside of the art school where she taught (La Cambre), and which are unfortunately very poorly documented. I was most interested in the work *Spontaneous Structure (Structure spontanée)*, a work that Tapta created in 1978 with her students from La Cambre for young children from a local school. As the title suggests, this was a spontaneous structure that was not executed according to Tapta's design, but it was entirely created by and through the participants' free gestures.

By reading about this work in scarce press clippings and listening to testimonies of Tapta's former student Ann Veronica Janssens, I wanted to understand how Tapta did pedagogy outside of the (art) school. The process of *Structure spontanée* shows that learning together can happen horizontally and in the absence of predetermined roles of teachers and students. Moreover, the premise of this project, a spontaneous structure without predetermined form, bears a lot of similarities with the methodologies behind *Felt workshops*.

How would you describe the relationship between your work and that of Tapta?

In my practice, I model woven textiles on photographs, which I use to document repairs and transformations in public spaces (*Materials* series, ongoing since 2015). I make use of the weaving process, which requires time and dedication, as a means of countering certain economic and social conditions, such as acceleration, standardization and transparency. The slow and caring work involved in weaving allows me to create new connections between working, thinking and feeling.

Beyond thinking about space and spatiality, I believe that there is a relationship between my hand-woven textiles and Tapta's so-called 'supple sculptures' through our manipulation of materials, which cannot only be looked at but also experienced in a more physical way.

In parallel to my weaving practice, I facilitate collaborative and participatory textile workshops, such as the *Felt workshops* mentioned above. This is yet another area which in my view has connections to Tapta's collaborative works such as *Structure spontanée* or *La Marolienne* (both of which were conceived in 1978). The latter project was never realized due to lack of budget. The sole remnant of that project is a model designed by Tapta and her La Cambre students for a playful community project for the (then) working-class Brussels neighborhood of De Marollen/Les Marolles. *La Marolienne*, imagined as an enormous structure of four cubic meters in the shape of a woman's body, sitting with her legs on a slope, was supposed to become an environment in which passers-by and local residents from all walks of life could play. Here again, I see a lot of similarities to processes and conditions that I care about in my own practice, such as the poetics and politics of public space, and its social connections.

What, in your opinion, is/was the importance of Tapta's practice? Why do you think Tapta's work is relevant today?

Tapta's modular and (re)moldable sculptures, whether they are made out of fiber, or neoprene and metal, and regardless of whether they were produced by her alone, with help from assistants in her studio, or in collaboration with groups of people, are not only flexible in terms of the material itself, but also conceptually and politically, as a result of their ability to activate the public, as well as the space that the sculptures themselves occupy, whether that is a gallery space or public space.

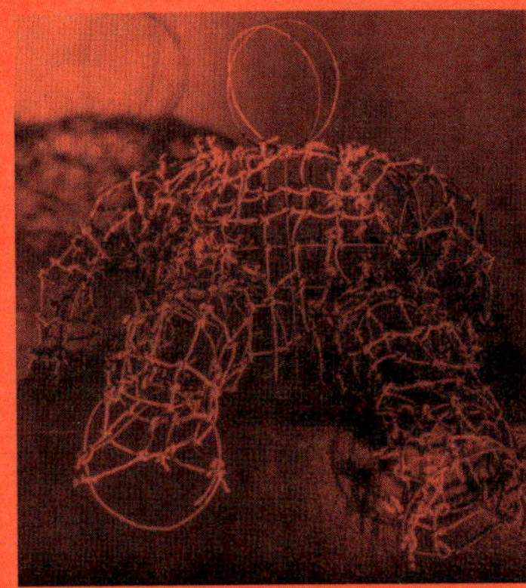

Scale model of *La Marolienne*, made by Tapta and her students of La Cambre in 1978. Photograph from Françoise Galle & Marie-Paule Ripoche, "Tapta" in *Dri a di*, 9, April 1979, p.19.

In my view, Tapta's works make ways for a multiplicity of spectators who can potentially transform into participants, or even co-makers of the work, and by doing so question the position of the singular author. In short, Tapta's work is still relevant today, due to the way that it is able to alter and accommodate the various social realities of the people interacting with and through her work.

Richard Venlet

What did you make for the exhibition?

The installation *Salon II*, which was developed in the context of the exhibition *Tapta: Espaces souples,* forms a continuation of an earlier work, *Salon I*, that I realized for the exhibition *Prelude: Melancholy of the Future* at the Museum Dhondt-Dhaenens in Deurle in 2020, and was reworked into a new configuration, specifically for this exhibition.

Salon II is a self-contained space that was constructed using a minimal number of materials and building elements. It consists of about thirty transparent plexiglass panels that are strung together using a simple connection principle that makes use of zip ties. Due to their specific method of attachment and positioning, the plexiglass panels form an organic and accessible self-supporting flexible exhibition structure.

As its title suggests, the installation forms a large representational space – or "salon", which can be accessed through three doorways. *Salon II* is designed as a sculptural transparent volume and nestles chameleonically as a room within the room. The work has the ambition and ability to facilitate and/or to be activated by different contents and uses. This activation takes place not only through its potential use but also through its own materiality when the transparency and light reflections blend into the context of the environment.

What was your starting point, or to which part of Tapta's practice does your work respond? How would you describe the relationship between your work and that of Tapta?

Within the exhibition *Tapta: Espaces souples*, *Salon II* negotiates a fluid and interactive interplay between the surrounding space, the strolling spectators, and the presented works by Tapta that are installed inside and around this transparent "salon". Form, sculpture, space, and the visitor's physical presence converge to form an overall experience in which tactile, spatial or visual boundaries become blurred. Like Tapta's more spatial works, such as *Transit* (1991) (p.76), *Salon II* seeks to engage in an active relationship with the viewer and encourages a quasi-organic connection towards what is shown. *Salon II* subtly forms and enlivens both the central space of the exhibition and the perception of the viewer, making their experience more physical and tangible.

Weaving, folding and hinging can be seen as a fundamental basic principle in creating flexible and fluid volumes, shapes and spaces. As within the work of Tapta, where intertwining

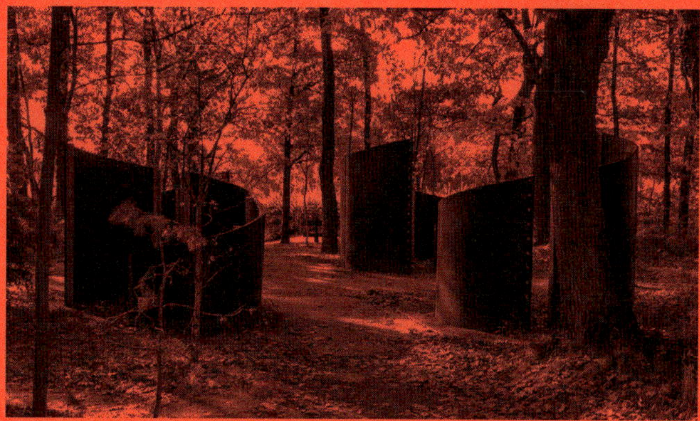

Tapta, *Transit* , 1991, neoprene and steel, pedestrian area of 1000 x 1000 cm, height from 40 to 200 cm. Open Air Museum of Sart Tilman, Liège

and bolting elements form the constructional core of her supple structures and sculptures, the hinge, which articulates the connection, is also an important design element within my own practice. In both of my spatial installations and hybrid scenographies, hinging is not only used to create a new and redirected perception on what is already there but it is also utilized in a more factual way, when I use hinges or zip ties to connect planes and sheet material into free architectural volumes such as *Salon II*.

What, in your opinion, is/was the importance of Tapta's practice? Why do you think Tapta's work is relevant today?

By presenting a compact overview of her works, the exhibition *Tapta: Espaces souples* demonstrated the importance and evolution of Tapta's artistic practice, in which weaving and connecting surfaces into spatial propositions — in addition to her role as a teacher and inspiration for later generations — occupied a central role.

The exhibition displayed and challenged Tapta's work by means of interventions by Greet Billet, Hana Miletić and myself. Based on our individual practices, interests and insights, the challenge was to further update the discourse surrounding Tapta's work and to re-examine it both artistically and critically. This exhibition project, as part of a broader research project, not only provided a concise overview of her practice, but also demonstrated, by confronting her heritage with contemporary practices, the significance of 'the actual exhibition' as an important artistic research methodology. Exhibitions such as *Tapta: Espaces souples* function as inspiring research platforms where new insights can be shared that result from and are created by artistic and critical practices.

It is not only Tapta's work that is the subject here, but rather a transhistorical belief that the confrontation and merging of past and present continually generates new and layered perspectives in which both the new and the foregoing can meet and be challenged.

78 List of Exhibited Works

p. 2–3, 4, 7, 9, 20
Tapta
La Chute de noeuds, 1970
Falling Knots
Cotton, wool, linen
230 x 165 cm
(Collection Maurice Verbaet)

p. 8–9, 11, 13
Tapta
Cocon n°1 et tapis spirale', 1973
Cocoon n°1 and spiral carpet
Cotton, sisal, carpet: linen or hemp
170 x 100 x 50cm/ ø 180 cm
(Belfius Art Collection)

p. 12, 15, 17, 24, 30
Tapta
Cocon n°2 et tapis spirale', 1973
Cocoon n°2 and spiral carpet
Cotton, sisal, carpet: linen or hemp
150 × 60 × 40 cm/ ø 180 cm
(Collection Musée d'Ixelles)

p. 12, 24, 27
Tapta
Untitled, 1973
Wool, sisal, wooden stick
225 x 100 x 6 cm (stick: 140 cm)
(Private Collection Antwerp)

p. 8, 29, 30
Tapta
Untitled (mobile), 1973
Wool, sisal, mixed fibres
ø 62 cm
(Private Collection)

p. 5, 9, 10, 14, 20
Tapta
Untitled (shawl), s.d.
Wool, mohair
175 x 114 cm
(Collection Maurice Verbaet)

p. 8, 10
Tapta
Untitled (shawl), s.d.
Wool, mohair, sisal, viscose
212 x 110 cm
(Collection Suzon Ingber)

p. 16, 18–19, 31
Tapta
Untitled, 1982
Wool and acrylic fibres
250 x 215 cm
(Private Collection Brussels)

p. 2–3, 4–5, 9, 14, 20–21
Tapta
Impatiente, 1995
Impatient
Neoprene and steel on wheels
Dimensions in folded form: 5 x 200 x 200 cm
(Collection BPS22, Charleroi)

p. 2, 9, 14, 21
Tapta
Untitled (Bertoia Diamond chair, covered with cords), s.d. (ca. 1980)
Metal, wool
(Collection Jean-Pierre Hoa)

p. 8, 13, 15
Tapta
Horizon flexible, 1977
Flexible Horizon
Wool, wood, plastic
ca. 230 x 225 x 75 cm
(Private Collection)

p. 54
Tapta
Untitled, 1994
Neoprene elements connected with hinges and metal base
63 x 34,5 x 5,2 cm (neoprene elements)
73 x 72 x 26 cm (base)
(Collection Maurice Verbaet)

p. 44–45, 46–47, 49, 51, 52–53
Tapta
Formes pour un espace souple
(partie de la réplique), 1974 (2023)
Forms for a Flexible Space (part of the replica)
Wool, cotton, metal rings
ca. 300 x 400 x 400 cm
(Collection M HKA)
Reconstruction process led by Chevalier-Masson studio, in association with Estelle Chatelain and Antonella Valerio, with the participation of students and volunteers from LUCA School of Arts and ENSAV La Cambre: Amaryllis Bouyer, Annelies Clerix, Bianca Cuevas Geiger, Rose Egidi, Coline Ernould, Sule Nur Eryuruk, Anouk Ostyn, Marie Rasper and Martha Verleyen.

p. 42–43, 53
Reconstruction studio where the replica of Tapta's *Formes pour un Espace Souple* was created during the exhibition.

Scale Models by Tapta

1st group (LEFT)

Tapta
Artelaguna (maquette), s.d. (ca. 1995)
Artelaguna (scale model)
Wood and sheet metal
11,5 x 34 x 5,5 cm
(Collection Maurice Verbaet)

Tapta
Untitled (scale model), s.d.
Neoprene and tape
10,2 x 35,5 cm
(Collection Maurice Verbaet)

Tapta
Untitled, 1986
Neoprene and metal
38 x 19,6 x 7 cm (1st piece)
28,5 x 17 x 7 cm (2nd piece)
(Collection Maurice Verbaet)

Tapta
Au bord du temps (maquette), 1990
On the Edge of Time (scale model)
Wood
10 x 33 x 5 cm
(Collection Maurice Verbaet)

Tapta
Untitled, 1991
Neoprene, bolts and nuts
27 x 57 x 10 cm
(Collection Maurice Verbaet)

Tapta
Untitled (scale model), s.d.
Neoprene and metal pins
7 x 19 x 5 cm
(Collection Maurice Verbaet)

Tapta
Untitled (scale model), s.d.
Neoprene and metal pins
5 x 20 x 9 cm
(Collection Maurice Verbaet)

Tapta
Untitled (scale model), s.d.
Neoprene, cardboard and screws
11 x 19,5 x 3,5 cm
8,5 x 16 x 3,5 cm
(Collection Maurice Verbaet)

Tapta
Untitled (scale model), s.d.
Neoprene, cardboard and pencil
4 x 20,5 x 14 cm
(Collection Maurice Verbaet)

Tapta
Untitled, s.d.
Neoprene and stone
18 cm x 72 cm x 8,5 cm
(Collection Maurice Verbaet)

Tapta
Untitled (scale model), s.d.
Neoprene, metal, screws
11,5 x 40 x 15 cm
10 x 40 x 12 cm
(Private Collection Brussels)

2nd group (MIDDLE)

Tapta
Structure élastique (maquette), 1981
Elastic Structure (scale model)
Rubber, glued on plywood
45,5 x 53 x 10 cm
(Collection Maurice Verbaet)

Tapta
Untitled, s.d.
Neoprene and metal pins
14 x 36 x 28 cm
(Collection Maurice Verbaet)

Tapta
Untitled, s.d.
Neoprene and metal pins
9,5 x 18 x 23 cm
(Collection Maurice Verbaet)

Tapta
Etude pour Chien de garde 2 (maquette), 1988
Study for Watchdog 2 (scale model)
Neoprene
47,5 x 68 (1st piece)
25 x 57,5 cm (2nd piece)
(Collection Maurice Verbaet)

Tapta
Néoflexible (maquette), 1985
Neoflexible (scale model)
Neoprene and wood
12,5 x 38 x 14 cm
10 x 40 x 12,5 cm
(Collection Maurice Verbaet)

Tapta
Horizon plastique (maquette), s.d. (ca. 1982)
Plastic Horizon (scale model)
Rubber
14,5 x 72 cm (1st piece)
10,5 x 60 cm (2nd piece)
(Collection Maurice Verbaet)

Tapta
Untitled (scale model), s.d.
neoprene
41 x 13 cm (closed)
(Private Collection)

Tapta
Untitled (scale model), s.d.
Neoprene, metal, screw clamp
37 x 124 x 58 cm
(Private Collection Brussels)

Tapta
Untitled, 1992
Neoprene connected by metal rod
15 x 29 x 5,2 cm
(Collection Maurice Verbaet)

3rd group (RIGHT)

Tapta
Untitled (scale model), 1991
Neoprene
18,5 x 60 cm
(Collection Maurice Verbaet)

Tapta
Lieu de transition, 1987
Place of transition
Neoprene, metal pins
ca. 13 x 40 x 40 cm
(Collection Maurice Verbaet)

Tapta
Untitled, s.d.
Neoprene and metal pins
ca. 9 x 33 x 12 cm
(Collection Maurice Verbaet)

Tapta
Portail oblique (maquettes), s.d.
Slanted Portal (scale models)
Sheet metal
2 x ca. 17 x 37 x 5,2 cm
(Collection Maurice Verbaet)

Tapta
Esprit ouvert, s.d. (ca. 1997)
Open Mind
Two metal elements connected by a rod and a stone base
60 x 31 x 6 cm (metal elements)
152 x 96 cm (base)
(Collection Maurice Verbaet)

Tapta
Untitled, s.d.
Neoprene, bolts and nuts
20 x 68 x 19 cm
(Collection Maurice Verbaet)

Tapta
Niké ou Projection de forces (maquette), 1987
Niké or Projection of forces (scale model)
Neoprene and cast stone
13,5 x 26,5 x 18 cm
(Collection Maurice Verbaet)

Tapta
Untitled (Segment d'une courbe), 1986
Untitled (Segment of a curve)
Neoprene and wood
15 x 11,5 x 4,5 cm
(Collection Maurice Verbaet)

Tapta
Angulaire (maquette), 1993
Angular (scale model)
Foam board connected by a rod
20 x 9 x 5 cm
(Collection Maurice Verbaet)

Greet Billet
Réfléchir (à) Tapta, 2023
two mirrors
2 x (430 x 230 x 487 x 0,6 cm)
Courtesy of the artist, galerie - EL, Welle, and Art Gallery De Wael 15, Antwerp

Hana Miletić
Felt workshops XII-XXI, 2022-2023 (ongoing)
Hand-made felts (raw wool in different colors) on steal backdrop stands
Dimensions variable
Collaboratively produced during public workshops facilitated by Hana Miletić, C'est la vie - Caritaszentrum Delbrêl and Frauen Aktiv Neustadt at Kunsthalle Mainz, and Espace Fxmme - Globe Aroma at Globe Aroma and WIELS, Brussels.
Courtesy of the artist, LambdaLambdaLambda, Prishtina, and The Approach, London

Richard Venlet
Salon II, 2023
Plexiglass
Dimensions variable
Courtesy of the artist